Celebrate
Memorial Day

by Melissa Ferguson

PEBBLE
a capstone imprint

First Facts are published by Pebble,
1710 Roe Crest Drive, North Mankato, Minnesota 56003
www.mycapstone.com

Library of Congress Cataloging-in-Publication Data
Library of Congress Cataloging-in-Publication data is available on the Library of Congress website.
978-1-9771-0266-9 (library binding)
978-1-9771-0530-1 (paperback)
978-1-9771-0283-6 (eBook PDF)

Editorial Credits
Mandy Robbins, editor; Cynthia Della-Rovere, designer; Pam Mitsakos, media researcher;
Tori Abraham, production specialist

Photo Credits
Alamy: National Geographic Creative, 19; Getty Images: Jeff Greenberg, 20–21, Philip James Corwin,
Cover, Sygma/Jeffrey Markowitz, 6–7; Newscom: Xinhua News Agency/Wang Ping, 17; Shutterstock:
Allen J.M. Smith, 13, Bokeh Blur Background, Design Element, Duda Vasilii, Design Element, Everett
Historical, 8–9, 10–11, Glynnis Jones, 4, sharpner, 1 (bottom), Zoran Karapancev, 3 (bottom left), 15

Printed and bound in the United States of America.
PA49

Table of Contents

What Is Memorial Day?

Americans celebrate Memorial Day the last Monday in May. For many people, this means enjoying a long weekend. But Memorial Day is important for a different reason. It's a time to honor *veterans* who have died in battle.

veteran—a person who served in the armed forces

4

People place flowers on graves to remember loved ones on Memorial Day.

Fact Memorial Day is different from Veterans Day. Veterans Day honors all U.S. veterans, past and present.

Memorial Day is a *federal* holiday. It honors military members who have died. People in the military help keep America safe and free. More than 1 million Americans have died in war since 1775.

Less than 10 percent of Americans are veterans.

federal—relating to the U.S. government

60 5673

How Memorial Day Became a Holiday

Memorial Day began after the Civil War (1861-1865). This war was a battle between America's northern and southern states. The states didn't agree on issues, such as states' rights and *slavery*.

Abraham Lincoln was president during the Civil War. He wanted America to stay a united country.

slavery—the owning of other people; slaves are forced to work without pay

Fact More soldiers died during the Civil War than in any other war in U.S. history.

The Battle of Shiloh was one of many battles fought during the Civil War.

Lincoln gave a speech during the Civil War called the Gettysburg Address. It honored the soldiers who had died.

The North won the war in 1865. America was united again. In 1868 Decoration Day began as a way to remember Civil War soldiers. People put flowers on soldiers' graves.

Lincoln gave the Gettysburg Address where Civil War soldiers were buried.

Over the next 100 years,
America fought in many wars.
Many men and women in the
military died. Americans wanted
a way to honor those who
died in these wars. Over time,
Decoration Day became known as
Memorial Day. In 1971 Memorial
Day became a federal holiday.

The Uniform Monday Holiday Act

Before 1968 Memorial Day was celebrated on May 30. In 1968 the government passed the Uniform Monday Holiday Act. This law moved some holidays, including Memorial Day, to a Monday. This change gave many American workers a long weekend.

Sites and Symbols of Memorial Day

Memorial Day has special *symbols*. One is the U.S. flag. The American flag is a symbol of freedom. *Wreaths* are another symbol of Memorial Day. Wreaths show respect for those who have died. Wreaths and flags are used to decorate the graves of U.S. veterans.

symbol—an object that stands for something else

wreath—a ring of flowers or branches; wreaths are often laid on graves or memorials

Memorial Day also includes the National Moment of Remembrance. This moment of silence is to remember those who died serving our country. The *tradition* started in 2000. At 3:00 p.m., *eastern time*, Americans join together in one minute of silent respect for soldiers who have died.

Arlington National Cemetery

Arlington National Cemetery is near Washington, D.C. More than 400,000 veterans are buried there. Each day, guards at the cemetery honor unknown soldiers who died in wars. On Memorial Day, there are large events to honor all soldiers who have died serving the country.

Special military ceremonies are held all over the country on Memorial Day.

tradition—a custom, idea, or belief passed down through time

eastern time—the time zone along the United States' east coast

How You Can Celebrate Memorial Day

Most people don't go to work or school on Memorial Day. They celebrate the holiday in many ways. People visit cemeteries and place flowers or wreaths on graves. Some communities hold parades or picnics. Others have speeches and concerts.

Fact During World War I (1914–1918), red poppies grew at the site of a bloody battle. Now red poppy flowers are often used to honor fallen soldiers.

You can honor those who died in wars too. You can go to a Memorial Day parade. Your family could visit a cemetery together. You could take a moment of silence to show you care on Memorial Day.

National Memorial Day Parade, in Washington D.C.

the Tuskegee Airmen who made the ultimate sacrifice for freedom in World War II

Glossary

cemetery (SEM-uh-ter-ee)—a place where dead people are buried

eastern time (EES-turn TYME)—the time zone along the United States' east coast

federal (FED-ur-uhl)—relating to the U.S. government

slavery (SLAY-vur-ee)—the owning of other people; slaves are forced to work without pay

symbol (SIM-buhl)—an object that stands for something else

tradition (truh-DISH-uhn)—a custom, idea, or belief passed down through time

veteran (VET-truhn)—person who served in the armed forces

wreath (REETH)—a ring of flowers or branches; wreaths are often laid on graves or memorials

Read More

Berne, Emma Carlson. *Memorial Day.* North Mankato, Minn.: Cantata Learning, 2018.

Koestler-Grack, Rachel A. *Memorial Day.* Celebrating Holidays. Minneapolis: Bellwether Media, Inc., 2018.

Lake, Kirsten. *Why Do We Celebrate Memorial Day?* Celebrating U.S. Holidays. New York: PowerKids Press, 2018.

Internet Sites

Use FactHound to find Internet sites related to this book.

Visit www.facthound.com

Just type in 9781977102669 and go.

Super-cool stuff!

Check out projects, games and lots more at
www.capstonekids.com

Critical Thinking Questions

1. Why do we celebrate Memorial Day?
2. How is Day different from Veterans Day?
3. What are two ways to honor veterans who died for our country?

Index

Otto & Daria

A Wartime Journey Through No Man's Land

Eric Koch

In memory of my mother,
my sister Margo,
and my brother Robert.

Printed and bound in Canada at Friesens.
COVER AND TEXT DESIGN: Duncan Campbell, University of Regina Press
COPY EDITOR: Meaghan Craven; PROOFREADER: Kristine Douaud
COVER PHOTO: "Practice" by Hannah Sorrells / Snapwire

Portions of the chapters "Refugees in the Blackout," "Tea with the Master," and "Internment: A Year in One Spot," were previously published in *I Remember the Location Exactly* (2006) by Mosaic Press, 1252 Speers Road Units 1 & 2, Oakville, ON, L6L 5N9. http://www.mosaic-press.com/product/i-remember-the-location-exactly/. Reprinted with permission.

Library and Archives Canada Cataloguing in Publication
Koch, Eric, 1919-, author
Otto & Daria : a wartime journey through no man's land / Eric Koch.

The book contains excerpts from letters by Eric Koch and Daria Hambourg. Issued in print and electronic formats. ISBN 978-0-88977-443-8 (hardback).— ISBN 978-0-88977-444-5 (pdf).— ISBN 978-0-88977-445-2 (html)

1. Koch, Eric, 1919— —Correspondence. 2. Hambourg, Daria—Correspondence. 3. World War, 1939-1945—Refugees—Canada—Biography. 4. Authors, Canadian (English)—20th century—Biography. 5. German Canadians—Biography. I. Title. II. Title: Otto and Daria.

PS8521.O23Z46 2016   C813'.6   C2016-903543-3   C2016-903544-1

University of Regina Press
Saskatchewan, Canada, S4S 0A2
TEL: (306) 585-4758   FAX: (306) 585-4699   web: www.uofrpress.ca

10   9   8   7   6   5   4   3   2   1

We acknowledge the support of the Canada Council for the Arts for our publishing program. We acknowledge the financial support of the Government of Canada. / Nous reconnaissons l'appui financier du gouvernement du Canada. This publication was made possible through Creative Saskatchewan's Creative Industries Production Grant Program.

Contents

Preface

THIS MEMOIR COVERS A PERIOD OF TEN YEARS, FROM 1938 to 1948. During this time, I was a refugee, a Jew forced to emigrate from Frankfurt, Germany, who eventually established roots in Canada, in Montreal and later Toronto.

The book contains excerpts from letters from Daria Hambourg, who, too, spent those years in limbo, but in a different sense. She was a member of a distinguished musical family in London but felt alienated from them. Throughout the war years, she moved from job to job and made a valiant attempt to find meaning in her life. This is reflected in her writing. While our experiences were different, what we had in common was that we were both young people caught up in the physical and psychological stress of the time.

Acknowledgements

THANKS ARE DUE TO MY DAUGHTER, MADELINE KOCH, for her editorial expertise, to my son, Tony Koch, for his computer assistance, to my friend, David Schatzky, who was the catalyst for the book after reading my collection of Daria's letters, and to my agent, Beverley Slopen, for her encouragement.

Acknowledgments

Meeting Daria

WHEN I MET DARIA SHE DIDN'T SAY A WORD. ALL SHE did was blush.

I was sitting in the lounge, waiting for lunch to be served. The date was August 7, 1938, a little more than a year before the outbreak of the Second World War, and the place the two-star Hotel Mirabeau in Champéry in the Swiss Alps, up the street from the five-star Grand Hotel. It was near the end of my summer vacation after my first year studying economics at the University of Cambridge. Adolf Hitler was threatening the world. But no one in the Hotel Mirabeau seemed to be aware of it.

Champéry, a famous skiing resort, was busier in the winter than it was in the summer. But now, in late August, the chairlifts took hikers to innumerable paths with splendid views of the multi-summited Dents du Midi. I preferred to stay in the hotel.

I had seen Daria at breakfast, the only other person in the dining room who was alone. She had lovely blue eyes, brown hair, a superb complexion, and was wearing a dark grey blouse. I discovered later that she was seventeen. She seemed perfectly happy reading a book.

A little later, lining up outside the dining room before lunch, Daria was standing with two other English girls, one of them called Angela and very forgettable. The other I had met the previous evening in the bar. Her name was Bea. She was flirtatious and attractive. Pursuing her, I thought, might well pay off. Both seemed to be chummy with a family called Wharry.

I rose to talk to Bea who remembered my name, which was promising. Admittedly, Otto is not a common name in England. She introduced me to Daria, who seemed shy but nodded and gave me a polite little smile. I bowed to her. I knew that English girls did not shake hands. I was wondering what she was doing in this hotel, also alone. Waiting for a grown-up to join her? I would probably find out later. For the moment I was more interested in Bea.

"Hungry?" Bea asked me.

"Not very."

"I suppose you're never hungry unless you know you're getting sauerkraut."

Daria poked her in the ribs.

"I have nothing against sauerkraut," Bea laughed.

She turned to me. "Did I say anything offensive, Otto?"

"Not at all," I replied, although I suspected she had noticed my accent and was going to tease me about being German. I had not told her I was a Jewish refugee.

"Are you a Nazi?" she asked me.

This time Daria poked her hard with her elbow. How interesting, I thought, a little puzzled. I looked at her face and noticed that she was blushing. Anger? Embarrassment?

"No, Bea." I spoke slowly, in an even voice. "I am not a Nazi."

"That's too bad," Bea replied. "I think the Nazis are much maligned in my country. My uncle attended one of those Nuremberg rallies and thought it was wonderful. He said one has to remember what a mess Germany was before Hitler came in."

This time Daria left without a word and threw herself on a leather armchair in the lounge.

"Strange girl," Bea said to me, shrugging. "Anyway, your sauerkraut should be ready by now."

Lo and behold, the doors opened. I let Bea and the others go into the dining room. I turned around and sat down on the side of Daria's chair.

"I think you made your point," I said to her. "I am very impressed. May I sit with you at lunch?"

"That would be nice," she said, careful not to sound too inviting. Those were the first words she spoke to me. For the next two days, once she had overcome her shyness, we spent most of the time together talking, in the lounge, during walks, or in the bar in the evening, drinking freshly pressed lemonade—never in each other's rooms. A dam had burst. Although she kept saying that she could express herself better on paper—she hoped to become a writer—she turned out to be an articulate, voluble, almost irrepressible talker. And she was magnificently English. I quickly forgot Bea.

Daria was by no means waiting for anybody to join her. She was killing time, waiting for her older sister, Sonia, to return to Paris, where she was living. Daria was going to stay with her for a few days, on the way home to London. Sonia was working as an editor for Albatross Press, Daria said. She had to meet an author somewhere in Normandy. She, Daria, had spent a week in Switzerland with one of her aunts, to celebrate her matriculation. I had got my matric after two years' residence at Cranbrook School in Kent, in the spring of 1937, a little more than a year before.

I was delighted to discover that she was the youngest of four daughters of the celebrated Russian-born concert pianist Mark Hambourg, whose recording of Beethoven's Concerto in C Minor I had often played on the portable gramophone I had with me in Cranbrook. I learned that her mother was the daughter of Sir Kenneth Muir Mackenzie, who had been—until his death in 1930—principal secretary of five successive lord chancellors. Daria's mother was the granddaughter of William Graham, MP, from Glasgow. She was a violinist universally known as Dolly, good enough to have studied with the great Eugène Ysaÿe in Belgium, the musician to whom César Franck had dedicated his violin sonata.

Daria gave me the family history without any shyness, more amused than boastful. I tried not to reveal how impressed I was. I wondered, of course, whether or not Mark Hambourg was Jewish, and if the reason Daria had poked Bea in the ribs was that she had guessed that I was Jewish and that therefore it was an expression of some kind of solidarity. Refugees like me were not used to consorting with granddaughters of lords and ladies and were therefore conditioned to cultivate "connections" outside Germany. But that was not—not consciously, anyway—the reason why I enjoyed my new friend so much. As I discovered later, Daria was not particularly interested in Jewish matters.

"What about you?" she asked.

"I'm from Frankfurt, and I'm going into my second year at Cambridge," I replied. "I am switching from economics to law."

"Oh, economics," she shuddered. "I am supposed to go to the LSE in the autumn." She was referring to the London

School of Economics. "I don't know why I allowed myself to be talked into that."

For the rest of our time together we discussed many things other than the joys of higher education. We could not know that this harmonious conversation would continue on paper for the next five years.

In 1995 I discovered a stack of Daria's letters in my desk in Toronto. They were sent to me between 1938 and 1943. Mine to her are lost. In 1938 Daria was seventeen, I eighteen.

I had not looked at the letters for decades. When I did so that year, I had an unexpected insight. Outward appearances notwithstanding, it seemed to me that our experiences were essentially the same. At that time, we were both passing through No Man's Land. My journey took me from the ruins of a shattered existence in Frankfurt, Germany, to the safe harbour of Canada. Daria's letters told a parallel story. They described vividly, often humorously, the road she travelled between a happy childhood and an unknowable future, and the mostly futile attempts she made to find herself, to carve out a role for herself.

Her story formed a counterpoint to mine.

CHAPTER I

Frankfurt: The Centre of the World

Es is kaa Stadt uff der weite Welt,
Die so merr wie mei Frankfort gefällt,
Un es will merr net in mein Kopp enei:
Wie kann nor e Mensch net von Frankfort sei!
[There is no city in the wide world
which pleases me as much as Frankfurt,
and it does not enter my head
how anybody could not have been born there.]
—FRIEDRICH STOLTZE, *"Frankfurt-Gedicht"*

THE FRANKFURT POET FRIEDRICH STOLTZE CON-
fessed—in local dialect and in verse—that he could not
imagine anybody not born in Frankfurt. He spoke for all
Frankfurters.

Frankfurt-centredness came naturally to us. It was not
easy for my uncles and aunts to welcome my sister Margo's
fiancé, who was born in Cologne. In the golden 1920s the

world considered Berlin the most exciting capital in the world, overflowing with advanced ideas. To Frankfurters it appeared vulgar and noisy. Having been born in 1919, I was, alas, too young to have an opinion on the subject.

The moral and intellectual superiority of Frankfurt was, of course, pure mythology. True, the city had been a financial and trade centre for centuries, and true, Frankfurt had been the place where coronations of Holy Roman Emperors took place, but it did not have a university until just before the First World War, and before the twentieth century it achieved little in the arts and sciences. Even then it was home to only one Nobel laureate, Paul Ehrlich, the father of chemotherapy, but he was not even born in Frankfurt. One celebrity who was, Goethe (1749–1832), perhaps the most admirable German who ever lived, left Frankfurt for Weimar when he was twenty-six, already the author of a bestseller, and only returned, not to see his mother, but to exchange poems with one of the many women he loved.

Mythology beats facts any day.

There is another celebrity who made Frankfurt famous—Mayer Amschel Rothschild (1744–1812). He was the founder of the Rothschild banking dynasty and was born in the ghetto, on the only street where Jews had been allowed to live since the Middle Ages. There was a curfew every evening, and the gates closed. The street was squalid and overcrowded. Rothschild never left the ghetto, even after he became rich. Throughout the nineteenth century, as its inhabitants became increasingly emancipated, the ghetto was gradually dismantled, and Jews were allowed to enter the larger community. My grandmother's grandfather lived down the street from Rothschild.

There was a painting of the "Jew Street" by Anton Burger in our dining room. In the 1960s a friend wrote to my mother, who was then living in New York, that he had seen it hanging in the leading art gallery in Hamburg. We thought it was an obvious case of art theft, somebody having stolen it from my mother during the hectic process of her emigration in early 1939. We were wrong. Burger painted a number of versions of the scene, perhaps hoping, with good reason, that people like my parents would buy one to remind themselves of where they came from. The Hamburg gallery had bought its version legitimately. Ours had disappeared.

My grandmother Flora Koch was born 1859 in Frankfurt's East End, no longer a ghetto. I remember her telling me that when she was seven the Prussians came and annexed the free city. The family fled to the nearby Taunus mountains, taking their silver spoons with them to save from the invaders. There was some resistance on the Hauptwache, the main square. One member of the Frankfurt militia was killed, and the mayor, Karl Viktor Fellner, committed suicide. A street is still named after him.

My grandmother's family moved to the West End at the end of the century, after her husband Robert Koch had established the jewellery firm to which we owed our good fortune. Thanks to his perseverance, good taste, and natural distinction—he looked like an ambassador—he became court jeweller, and his store became a Frankfurt version of Tiffany's or Cartier's. The location was less than one block away from Frankfurt's "Ritz," the Frankfurter Hof. Robert Koch's rise to prominence coincided with the boom following German reunification in 1871.

Robert was born in Geisa, a small town not far from Frankfurt, the son of a country doctor who had died in 1870. His penniless widow, referred to in the family as Grandmama Doktor, moved to Frankfurt hoping to find suitable wives for her four sons in the Jewish community that had emerged from the ghetto. She was not disappointed. Her one daughter, a gifted pianist, however, slipped away; she married a Hungarian adventurer and moved to Paris.

Two of Grandmama Doktor's four sons, Karl and Fritz, went into business but failed to achieve spectacular success because they were more interested in "higher things," namely intellectual and scientific pursuits. The other two, Robert and Louis, struck it rich as upper-echelon jewellers. Robert's oldest son was my father, Otto, who died in 1919 when I was three months old. He served as an absent role model for my brother and me throughout our childhood.

It was only natural that Frankfurt's magnetism attracted upwardly mobile people from everywhere. My mother's banking family, the Kahns, came from Steppach, a little village near Heilbronn, in the state of Baden. Her great-grandfather Michael had discovered around 1840 that there was a demand for bed feathers. Before that, only the nobility and the rich could afford to sleep in soft feather beds. Old Kahn processed feathers and democratized sleep. This activity was rudely interrupted by the Revolution of 1848. Two of his young sons, Bernhard and Hermann, who helped in the family business, were idealistic radicals who participated in the fighting. When the Prussians came to put down the revolution, Bernhard managed to escape across the Swiss border and made his way to Albany, New York, where he stayed for ten years and learned something about banking. Hermann, my great-grandfather, stayed behind. He was caught and tried. He was not amnestied until his enterprising mother, Franziska, the daughter of the Löwenwirt Baer, the owner of the Lion Tavern, went to the capital Karlsruhe to visit the grand duke to plead for his life. After being thrown out several times, she finally got through. The grand duke was kind and respectful. She described this achievement in a diary written in imperfect German.

From feathers, via revolution, to banking was only a small step. The Kahns became established in Mannheim a generation before the Kochs in Frankfurt. My great-grandfather Hermann, who had opened a branch of the bank in Frankfurt, died before I was born. It would have been hard to imagine that the distinguished, bearded old gentleman I knew from pictures had been a hothead in his youth. Evidently banking came more naturally to the Kahns than revolution, or, for that matter, bed feathers. They became patrons of the arts and literature. Today the public library of Mannheim still has a reading room they endowed in memory of Bernhard. There was a lot of music in their house. When Brahms visited Mannheim, he stayed there. The family's role in Mannheim is described in several biographies of Otto H. Kahn, one of Bernhard's sons, who went to New York around the turn of the twentieth century, made a killing on Wall Street, and became one of the founders of the Metropolitan Opera. It was partly thanks to him that Caruso and Toscanini came to New York. When necessary, he also covered the Met's deficit out of his own pocket. His summer house on the North Shore of Long Island had 127 rooms and served F. Scott Fitzgerald as inspiration for Gatsby's house in *The Great Gatsby*.

Although a banker's daughter, my mother was not really suited to be a jeweller's wife and did not enjoy the Kochs' dependence on wealthy customers. However, the Kochs made a point of never being obsequious to the rich and powerful. For Uncle Louis, the head of the family after Robert's death in 1902, my mother was not grand enough.

Indeed, she was not grand at all: her tastes were intellectual and bookish. She had been brought up in a comfortable house, the oldest of three children, in Frankfurt's West End. The expectation was for her to marry and let her future husband be in charge. When she finished her education after one year in Brussels, at a finishing school for "girls of good family," her inclination was to go to university. Only a few girls in her circle managed that, however, and she was not strong-willed or confident enough to run against the stream.

My mother grew up on the Niedenau, just south of the Bockenheimer Landstrasse, a major artery between the opera and the western suburbs. The Kochs' apartment was on the Unterlindau, just north of the Bockenheimer Landstrasse, less than ten minutes away. I know nothing about my parents' courtship, nor whether they ever met as children or teenagers. The only documentary evidence I have of their early lives is a letter Otto wrote to Ida soon after they met, written in surprisingly formal and respectful language. My mother had kept it. This has always surprised me, since I have never seen a single letter he wrote to her during the war.

The thing I do know about is the precise moment they became engaged. My mother was a good pianist, and my father a more than competent violinist, probably better than I was. They were playing Beethoven's Spring Sonata, which, a generation later, I also played with my mother. At the end of the slow movement there is a counterintuitive shift in rhythm where one can easily lose one's place. They did. And so did I, several times. On one of these occasions, my mother told me, "This is the spot where your father and I became engaged."

In 1911 Otto Koch married Ida Kahn, and they took an apartment not far from where they were brought up. Many descendants of the ghetto found their way to the West End, but in our high school, no more, probably less, than 10 per cent of the boys were Jewish. Refugees from pogroms in Russia and Poland settled in the East End, but we had no contact with them. We had little sense of Jewish solidarity and organized religion played a subordinate role in our lives. We did not go to school on Yom Kippur. At Christmas we had a Christmas tree. Only on the High Holidays did we go to the synagogue. Our social life was mostly with assimilated Jews like ourselves. Twice a week at school, a Jewish scholar taught us Jewish history and the meaning of Jewish holidays while the Protestant and Catholic boys learned the rudiments of their religions. This was not mandatory. Atheists could opt out and play football.

Frankfurt did not attract only bankers. After the First World War the philosopher Franz Rosenzweig came to Frankfurt and established the Jüdische Lehrhaus, a project in adult education to acquaint the increasingly alienated

Jewish inhabitants of the West End with the treasures of the Jewish tradition in order to reverse the drift away from Judaism. (Rosenzweig and the writer Martin Buber joined forces to translate the Hebrew Bible into German. One semi-jocular critic thought the result sounded like Wagner's *Der Ring des Nibelungen*.) The Lehrhaus had no *Haus* of its own but conducted lectures and seminars in private residences. Some members of my family supported this initiative, but others were more interested in the neo-Marxists and Freudians identified with the Frankfurt School at the University's Institute for Social Research, such as Herbert Marcuse, Theodore Adorno, and Max Horkheimer.

Not only bankers and scholars flocked to Frankfurt but so, too, did musicians. In 1927, to observe the centenary of Beethoven's death, the city staged an international music exhibition and a summer of music on a lavish scale. It was an occasion for the performances of many new works, from all over the world. The Frankfurt Opera performed all the operas Richard Strauss had composed up to that point. It was the first time since the war that Germans and their former enemies could, in Goethe's liberal spirit, once again participate as equals. Germany was being readmitted to the civilized world.

This was Frankfurt-centredness at its best.

CHAPTER 2

St. John's Wood

IN HER LETTERS DARIA RARELY MENTIONED HER FAMily, but when I wrote *The Brothers Hambourg*, a book about her father and his three brothers, I found the answers to many of the questions I wanted to ask her but never had the opportunity.

When she was born in 1920, Mark Hambourg was forty and his great days as a piano virtuoso were over. He was born in 1879 in the village of Boguchar on the Don River, halfway between Moscow and the Black Sea. He was taught by his father Mikhail Hambourg, a noted piano teacher who had studied with Nicolai Rubinstein and Sergei Taneyev at the Conservatoire in Moscow. He was a child prodigy. In 1889, when he was ten, his father took him to London, not speaking a word of English, hoping that Mark would have a greater career in the West than he would have at home. Two years later, the thirty-five-year-old music critic George Bernard Shaw heard Mark play and wrote that "he might astonish the world some day but he does not seem to be exactly on the way of getting it at present." But Shaw got to know the boy quite well and "detected that his charm in private intercourse was that he betrayed the heart of an affectionate child behind a powerful and very lively intellect."

The family settled in Bloomsbury, the home of many Russian émigrés, among them the legendary anarchist Prince Kropotkin, whom Daria quoted twice in her letters. A year or two after Shaw, Paderewski heard Mark play, was greatly impressed by his talent but recognized that he needed more training than his father could give him. So he and a few others funded studies with the doyen of all piano teachers at the time, Theodor Leschetizky in Vienna, a student of Carl Czerny, himself a student of Beethoven. A few students of Leschetizky, Artur Schnabel for one, made the transition to contemporary tastes. Mark was not among them.

Mark studied with Leschetizky for four years. After his return to England in the spring of 1895, he launched a career of a special kind. In a number of concert tours, he brought classical music to remote parts of the British Empire. Locals carried pianos on their backs so that he could play Liszt's Hungarian rhapsodies to amazed audiences in the jungle. (Malicious critics said that he was the loudest pianist in the British Empire.) He also toured in the United States and Canada. In 1916 Mark's parents and three brothers moved to Toronto, but his father died soon after their arrival.

Daria and her three older sisters grew up in a home in London's St. John's Wood. In an obituary in the December 22, 2004, *Independent*, Martin Anderson quotes Daria's sister Michal, who described their home as "full of music and musicians. In the evenings, after dinner, everyone played chamber music and I have only to close my eyes to feel the experience of intense life and energy in that musical scene. Many of the great musicians of those days were my parents' friends. Busoni, Paderewski, Rubinstein, Huberman, Piatigorsky, Rachmaninoff, Friedman, Moiseiwitsch, and many others, all came and made music." The Hambourgs were used to a lively social life, and not only with musicians. Daria told me that her maternal grandfather, Sir Kenneth Muir Mackenzie, had had many guests. A widower, he lived with the Hambourgs until his death in 1930 at the age of eighty-four, when Daria was ten. When I read Mark Hambourg's memoirs, I learned that his father-in-law had been a friend of "Bishops, Cabinet Ministers, Lord Chancellors, Diplomats, Generals, Heroes, and Mr. Winston Churchill as a young man."

In one of her early letters to me, Daria describes her upbringing.

August 15, 1938
I had, unfortunately for biographical purposes, an
exceedingly happy childhood and was understood
perfectly by all who cared to understand me, being
much given to doll-washing, eating of sweets when
permitted and occasionally when not permitted,
dressing up, showing off, fighting Michal, and—
dancing! I believed for many years in spite of my better self in the Fairy Queen, corresponded annually
for profit with Father Christmas, and acquired an
unusually intelligent canary and, later, a dog. I defy
you, even under the most pressing circumstances, to
start a biography with such scanty material.

Michal was one year older than Daria and the only one of
Mark's four daughters who became a remarkable pianist
and teacher herself. For that reason, as she grew up, her
relationship with her father was particularly close. She had
been a regular visitor to the recording studios since the age
of eight, acting as her father's page-turner. At the age of
fourteen, she made a recording with him of Schumann's
two-piano *Andante and Variations*, and Liszt's *Concerto
Pathétique*. They both played from memory. According
to her obituary, a seasoned observer felt that her playing
brought out the best in her father's.

In the 1930s Michal toured Britain with singers of the stature of Paul Robeson, Lawrence Tibbett, and Richard Tauber. In her letters to me, Daria described Michal's appearance at the Proms in 1938, playing Saint-Saëns's *Piano Concerto no. 5* under the baton of Sir Henry Wood.

September 14, 1938
Michal's concert, which you expressed a wish to hear about, was an unqualified success. I pushed my way into the very front of the "Prom" part of the hall and stood in the shadow of Sir Henry Wood's frenzied arm, just beneath the orchestra, so that when she appeared, looking serene, grave and rather aloof, her eye caught mine and she smiled, whereas I, unaccountably, blushed.

I will describe to you her appearance, because I know you appreciate beautiful things. She is, as you know, tall and pale with dark hair and dark eyes, and she wore a very simple white dress, falling straight from her shoulders to her waist and then standing out stiffly in a sort of hoop. You can imagine the effect in a dim hall, when she swept through the serried ranks of black and white orchestra and fat old women in lace gowns!

They played the Saint-Saëns Concerto in C minor, how well I cannot say, partly because I was too excited and partly because I love music so much that, so long as it is at least competently interpreted I lose all critical faculties in listening to it. This is not an affectation, although my family, thinking as they do that I hate music—an impression I am not at any pains to correct—would certainly believe that it is.

Afterwards there was a party. When I met you in Switzerland I was bored with social functions, despised them, feared and also hated them. Now they seem utterly and entirely unimportant as do all such things. The clothes, the manners, the polite gossip—I have become indifferent and even tolerant towards them.

Soon after the concert Michal married the architect Edward Lewis.

During the war Michal performed in Myra Hess's wartime series of lunchtime recitals in the National Gallery. She was a frequent performer on the BBC, too, sometimes in the company of Dylan Thomas.

But not long after the war she turned her back on the limelight. During a concert tour of South Africa, an Anglican priest asked her to fit in an extra performance for his black parishioners who were barred from the concert halls.

Never, she said, had she had such an appreciative and attentive audience. From that time on she determined to offer support and help to young musicians in need. The foundation of the National Association for Gifted Children (NAGC) gave her a framework for her work as a music counsellor.

Michal's marriage to Edward Lewis was a failure. Her happy second marriage, which lasted over half a century, was to Ian MacPhail, a founder of the World Wildlife Fund. Their son Rob survived them.

The last few years of Michal's life, as reported in her obituary, were marked by an improbable return to international prominence as a player. Allan Evans, whose CD label Arbiter specialized in historical recordings, was putting together a program of Mark's performances. He discovered the duo performances with Michal. Was she still alive, Evans wondered, and if so, where? He made some inquiries. Soon a letter arrived from Rob MacPhail, announcing that his mother was indeed well, and in fine pianistic form, having maintained a rigorous schedule of domestic practice. Rob arranged for a recording engineer to visit. More than sixty years after those first sessions, Michal Hambourg resumed her recording career.

For Evans, who worked with her for nine years, her playing represented a unique synthesis of the late nineteenth century's use of touch and colour, and a modern, heightened understanding of structure and style, making her a unique amalgam of two worlds.

Daria's other two sisters, Nadine, born in 1911, and Sonia, born in 1908, were rarely mentioned in Daria's letters. Nadine became the second wife of the social scientist Thomas Humphrey Marshall, who did his best, without much success, to arouse Daria's interest in economics. He was a Fellow of Trinity College, Cambridge, and became well-known in particular for his essay on citizenship and social class, published in 1950. He died in 1981. From 1939 to 1944, Marshall was head of the Social Science Department at the London School of Economics, which shortly after the beginning of the Second World War was evacuated to Cambridge. Daria visited Nadine and her brother-in-law in Cambridge once during the winter of 1939–40, while I was there.

Early November, 1938
It may be impossible for me to see you in Cambridge, because of staying as a guest in other people's houses. I don't know the Marshalls' plans, and whether or not they would be offended if I produced ones of my own. I don't want to meet you on ceremonious footing amongst a large gathering of unknown people, as I find this embarrassing.

I found this explanation entirely plausible and did not mind at all. I was too involved in my own work and activities to be disappointed. I did not feel Daria was under any obligation to make a special effort to see me.

I did not become acquainted with Nadine until more than half a century later when, accompanied by my daughter Madeline, I interviewed her in Cambridge for my book on her father and three uncles. A large oil painting of Mark dominated the foyer of her house. In addition to the invaluable information she gave me about her family, she told me the story of her older sister Sonia, born in 1908, twelve years before Daria.

Nobody less than a future prime minister of England, Nadine told us, would have been worthy of the brilliant and beautiful Sonia, her parents thought. However, when she went to Oxford she fell in love with a young poet. (That was probably Clere Parsons, whose work was influenced by W.H. Auden and Laura Riding.) The parents disapproved. They told her to wait. Sonia waited. In the end, in 1931, they gave in. A wedding was arranged, but before it could take place the young man died of pneumonia at the age of twenty-three. Sonia was shattered, devastated. She went to Paris to work for Albatross Press, founded in 1932, originally a German publishing house based in Hamburg. It produced the first modern, mass-market paperbacks. In

Paris, Sonia edited *The Albatross Book of Living Prose* and *The Albatross Book of English Humour*.

In 1940 the Germans came. The family assumed Sonia had been, in Nadine's words, "swallowed by the Holocaust." But she survived. It seems she had married. Nadine could only tell us that her husband did not survive. At some stage during the Nazi occupation, Sonia took refuge in the Maison des Soeurs in Bussy-en-Othe in Burgundy, not far from Dijon, where, as a member of the Russian Orthodox sisterhood, she spent the rest of her life under the name of Mère Marie.

Not long after my conversation with Nadine, Madeline and I visited the Maison while we were on holiday in France. Nadine had given us the address. We spoke to the mother superior. She told us that Mère Marie had died a few years earlier after having translated the service books of the Russian Orthodox Church into English. The bishop had taken the credit. We spoke in French, and I cannot recall her exact words. It was Mère Marie's version, the nun said, that was now used in Russian Orthodox churches in the English-speaking world. She showed us a silver-framed photograph of Mère Marie. I thought she looked like her father.

Finally, the nun told us something quite remarkable. Mère Marie had been highly respected by everybody, she said, especially by the people on the land with whom she worked.

One reason for that respect was that they had heard that in Paris, under the Occupation, Mère Marie had helped so many Jews.

CHAPTER 3

Westendplatz

WE—MARGO, MY BROTHER ROBERT, AND I—GREW
up in the heart of Frankfurt's West End, within easy walking distance of our schools and our two widowed grand-
mothers. My brother was only fifteen months older than
I. We were treated as twins and shared a Prussian but
amiable governess, Fräulein Annelies, the daughter of a
ship's captain in Bremen. Our sister was born in 1912, seven
years before me, and was therefore, as far as we were concerned, grown up.

Our parents had moved into our comfortable but unos-
tentatious first-floor apartment near the Westendplatz in
1911 when they married. Our mother lived there until her
emigration. For her, the first three years of marriage were
idyllic, as they must have been for our father, whom I
did not know. All this came to an end in 1914. My father
became an officer in 1915, a rare event for a Jew so early

in the war. Later, many others followed. Some years later a story about my father's promotion appeared in Martin Buber's monthly publication *Der Jude*.

Otto was an enthusiastic horseman. Before 1914 he and a friend owned a stable in the municipal forest, where he went for practice sessions most mornings before going to sell pearl necklaces, diamond rings, and sapphire broaches to his faithful customers at the Robert Koch store near the Frankfurter Hof. One of their horses was named Never Mind: I remember as a child wondering what that English phrase meant. As a competitor in horse-jumping tournaments, he established a record of two metres in 1913, which was broken only in 1927 by Baron von Buddenbrock. Engraved silver trophies of his triumphs decorated our apartment. He dislocated his shoulder during a fall before the war and decided if he survived he would try to get it repaired as soon afterwards as possible. He tried, but the ensuing surgery in 1919 went wrong, and he died of a sepsis. Today an antibiotic would have taken care of it.

My mother was twenty-nine and never recovered. Until old age—she died in Washington in 1981 at the age of ninety-one—it was almost impossible for her to talk about him as it was difficult for her to communicate her feelings generally, both in conversation and in writing. The shadow of his death hung over our childhood.

Thanks to our jewellery store, however, we never had any money problems, even during the Depression. People bought jewels in those years, among other reasons, because they were safe investments. As children, however, we rarely saw the world of grown-ups. Their world and ours did not overlap. I remember once, when I was about twelve, I went downtown with my mother. An elderly gentleman greeted her. I asked, "Who was that?" She answered, not unkindly, "You don't know him." She was telling me in so many words to postpone crossing the line between my sphere and hers until it was absolutely necessary. The adult world was not much fun for anybody, she implied. My mother was protecting me. If there had been battles between Communists and Nazis on the Westendplatz—there were none—we children would not have known about it unless we had witnessed it. But after 1933, when the Nazis took power and swastikas were everywhere, we knew the enemy had taken over. Not long ago, speaking at a school, my New York cousin, Wolf Kahn—he was only six in 1933—referred to the children's insulation from horror in those years. He called his speech, ironically, "My Happy Days under the Nazis." Not everybody grasped the irony.

In the late 1920s, after years of relative seclusion, my mother fell in love again, with Emil Netter. She married him in 1930. Naturally this was a major event in our lives, entirely positive. We liked him immensely, and he was good with us. Emil was different from my father—an industrialist, imposing, dynamic, moody, unusually well-read and far more interested in Jewish matters than my father had been. When they married, my stepfather was thirty-eight, two years younger than my mother. Born in Strasburg, he was a partner in Wolf Netter and Jacobi, a large metal-processing company, founded by his grandfather in 1833, in Bühl, a small town near Baden-Baden in the Black Forest. (Curiously, my maternal grandmother came from the same town, which had a substantial Jewish community.)

The Netters manufactured, in various plants, corrugated iron and diverse steel products such as book shelves and garbage cans. In 1873, after the Franco-Prussian War, the company moved across the Rhine to Alsace, which had become German. In 1905 it had three thousand employees and was the largest enterprise of its kind in Europe. When, in 1918, Alsace became French again, the company lost 80 per cent of its assets. The Netters could have stayed, but they chose to move to Germany where the family had originally come from. The administration moved to Berlin and Frankfurt.

Emil had two younger sisters. All three had tuberculosis. It was not clear how they were infected. Emil became ill in 1913. Cecile died in 1915, and Helene in 1922. Emil spent ten years in a sanatorium in Davos, Switzerland, occasionally close to death. When he was contemplating marriage to my mother, five years after his discharge, he took her to see his former doctors to obtain their approval. They gave it. Looking back, as things turned out, I think they should have withheld it.

He was not as robust as they—and he—thought he was. He had not regained his strength sufficiently to be able to cope with the world after 1933, when the Nazis came to power. Soon it became clear that he should emigrate. One option was Palestine. He was sufficiently interested in Zionism to send sections of his library to the new Hebrew University in Jerusalem, which needed books. But he was not up to making the decision to go there.

Toward us three children, Emil Netter was always an exemplary stepfather, but after three years of marriage he found it intolerable that my mother continued to be attached to the Koch family and remain a silent partner in the Koch store. The marriage suffered. There were many agonizing quarrels.

On a Sunday morning in February 1936—by then I was in school in England—he killed himself in his office. (He had borrowed a gun from a loyal employee because Jews were not allowed to own firearms.) In 1938, two years after his death, when the Netter company was taken over by the Nazis, his partners took their losses and somehow managed to leave. No doubt he could have done this, too, if he had been well enough. My mother was paralyzed by his suicide. Her letters to me were barely decipherable.

After 1933 the full horror of things to come was not foreseeable, but many Jews who grasped the danger left. Margo went to Paris early in 1934 and found a job in a Flammarion book store. I visited her on my Easter holidays. Some time afterwards she met Paul Mayer. He had just finished his education in Cologne to become a lawyer, but of course, being Jewish, was not allowed to practise. He went to Paris. But he could not get permission to work there—he needed a *carte de travail*, which was granted to few refugees—and returned to Germany to prepare himself to emigrate to the United States. In 1936, three months after Emil Netter's death, Paul and Margo married in Frankfurt. While waiting for a visa, they took an apartment in Cologne.

Robert went to a commercial school in Lausanne, Switzerland, and in 1937 left for New Orleans where distant relatives had just been discovered. The circumstances were bizarre. Dorche, the gifted pianist and the sister of our paternal grandfather, had married an adventurous Hungarian, whom we called the Pirate for some reason. The descendants of the Pirate and his first wife lived in New Orleans and were very kind to Robert. He got a job in an export business, which, considering the Depression, was an enormous achievement.

Money could not be taken out of Germany. Still, many Jewish parents who were in a position to finance the schooling of their children abroad somehow managed to do so. Mine did. In March 1935, a year before his death, Emil Netter and my mother took me to London, where we stayed for three days in the posh Park Lane Hotel on Piccadilly. Later that year, I went to Cranbrook School, Kent.

It was my entry into No Man's Land.

CHAPTER 4

The Playing Fields of Cranbrook

"THE BATTLE OF WATERLOO WAS WON ON THE PLAYing fields of Eton," the Duke of Wellington is supposed to have said. In the hierarchy of English public schools (meaning not paid for by the state) whose alumni ran the British Empire, which still existed in 1935, Eton was the top and Cranbrook near the bottom. I have no idea what school Daria went to. We never talked about it, but I do remember telling her about Cranbrook because the school transformed me from being a German schoolboy to being a refugee schoolboy. It had received a royal charter from Queen Elizabeth I in 1574. When I left in 1937, after two years, I was told by my house master, a historian, that I had been the worst house prefect since Queen Elizabeth. More about him later.

One of the many charms of Cranbrook was that it was on the outskirts of an unspoiled village dominated by an imposing windmill, located in the pleasantly undulating, hops-growing countryside of Kent. It was not far from the Sissinghurst estate of Harold Nicolson, who spoke to us once on Speech Day, and Vita Sackville-West. The school had boarders like me and day-boys from Cranbrook and the neighbouring villages. We all had to wear either school or house ties, but not uniforms. There was a middle-aged "matron," Miss Rowntree, who looked after us when we were sick, sewed on our buttons, and gave us dancing lessons in the dormitories.

At times I was homesick, but the boys did their best to make my transformation surprisingly painless. I was never teased for being foreign, except when they noticed a large German sausage in my tuck box. If I was indeed a terrible house prefect, this may have been due to the minor detail that I never understood what a house prefect was supposed to do. Cane little boys for talking after lights-out in the dormitories? (Caning was one of my privileges, not duties.) Or for not polishing my shoes properly when they were my "fags" (personal servants to older boys). (Little Churchill had been a fag to bigger boys at Harrow.) Or for not opening the door for me? There were some evident differences between the value systems of Cranbrook and those of the Goethe Gymnasium, my high school in Frankfurt. I could never understand why to be "brainy" was considered a vice rather than a virtue. In Frankfurt I was pleased on the rare occasions when I got a good mark, say, in Latin. At Cranbrook a triumph on the playing field was more praiseworthy.

I must have seemed very odd to the boys when I arrived: the only foreigner at the school. There was no need for me to advertise that I was Jewish as well as foreign. In my first year I went to chapel on Sundays and sang hymns (I still like them), but in my second year, when I was joined by another Jewish refugee from Germany—I couldn't stand him, he broke my monopoly—we were excused from chapel. My English, feeble at the start, was improving. I had learned French, Latin, and Greek in the Goethe Gymnasium, but not English. But before leaving Frankfurt I had had private English lessons, and in the spring of 1935, after my parents had delivered me to England to start at Cranbrook in the fall, I went to Croydon, south of London, to spend the summer with the Parkinson family, who had been hosts to Margo for six months in 1932. I think Emil Netter had found them. He could not have done better. Both Margo and I remained in touch with the Parkinsons for years. They were ideally suited to teach me English and English-ness. In Frankfurt's smug West End, we had not known families who were as welcoming to strangers as the Parkinsons were to Margo and me. The Reverend George Parkinson was a Methodist minister conditioned to be kind to fellow humans who were uprooted. Mrs. Parkinson was pleasant and generous, and so were their four children, George (Junior), Muriel, Joyce, and Christine. Their library cards were in a glass jar on the mantelpiece in the living room. In Frankfurt I didn't know what a public library was. Nor did I know bacon and eggs, shepherd's pie, savouries, and what they called puddings. Or the ubiquitous tea.

C.O.C. Osborne, the brilliant master of Cranbrook's Cornwallis House, the man who made me house prefect and later pretended to regret it, was similarly kind and similarly understanding of my situation. He was extraordinary—a dwarf with a big egg-like head on top of a tiny body and a face with little pink apple-cheeks like Punch. He was universally known as Pop. No German boys would have taken to a miniature edition of a man like him. He governed by force of personality and intellect. Also, he was an anti-imperialist socialist, which appealed to me even then. The Duke of Wellington would not have approved.

Music was not taught. By the time I had left Frankfurt I had had three years of violin lessons and enjoyed playing sonatas with my mother, a good pianist. I was no prodigy. I have always been a good third-class violinist. But I missed it at Cranbrook. It so happened that the headmaster, C.S. Scott, also played the violin, very well. Pop told him about me. The headmaster was a remote figure with whom I had never exchanged a word. One day he sent a boy to ask me whether I would like to play the Bach double concerto with him in his living room, with his wife at the piano. I was amazed, excited, and immensely pleased. It went very well. Strangely enough, I was not nervous at all. I knew the concerto and did well enough for him to arrange with the headmistress of nearby Benenden School—a *girls'* school—to join their orchestra on Wednesday afternoons while other boys played cricket. I went there by bicycle, for several weeks. We played the *Capriol Suite* by Peter Warlock. I still remember every note. As to the boys I left behind at Cranbrook: I enjoyed being envied. At Benenden, the only conversation I had with a girl was short and began with the question, "Who will turn the page, you or I?"

Other conversations I had in my two years at Cranbrook were more rewarding, mostly those with Pop. He was by far the best teacher I ever had. In my second year he arranged a trip to Oxford for me to sit for an exam for a scholarship to study history at Balliol, his old college. I went there but did not succeed. I was not upset. I had not expected I would. But Pop thought the experience would be good for me. I subsequently received a nice letter from Balliol encouraging me to try again. It did not come to that. The headmaster wanted me to go to his old college, St. John's at Cambridge, which I managed to do without a scholarship. Only in my last year did I run into money difficulties.

Pop's concern for me and my situation went as far as to convey to the Home Office, after he heard about my stepfather's suicide, that he would be prepared to employ my mother as a housemaid in case she needed such a commitment for a visa to immigrate to England.

Fortunately, she was able to make other arrangements.

CHAPTER 5

Shadows of the Past

I LEFT CRANBROOK IN THE SPRING OF 1937 BUT DID not meet Daria until August 1938. While I was in my school she was in hers.

During my two years at Cranbrook I regularly went back to Frankfurt on my holidays, despite the Nazis. Curiously, although I was already a refugee, I still had one toe in Nazi Germany because my mother was still there and there was no need to formalize my exit. There seemed to be no danger and the fares could be paid in German money. I never had any trouble.

I went to Frankfurt again in the spring of 1937 after leaving Cranbrook. My first term at St. John's College, Cambridge, would not begin until the fall. My mother was in bad shape but was slowly regaining her balance. Robert was getting ready to leave for the United States. Before saying goodbye, we spent a few melancholy days with her in Baden-Baden, the historic resort that had played such a major role in the Koch family's past. (It also triggered my novel *Earrings,* published by Mosaic Press in 2001.) It was in fashionable Baden-Baden that my handsome grandfather Robert Koch, after opening a modest jewellery store in the East End of Frankfurt in 1879, charmed the Duchess of Hamilton. She was the daughter of Stephanie, the Grand Duchess of Baden and niece of Alexandre de Beauharnais, who was the first husband of Napoleon's Josephine and was guillotined in 1794. The duchess's salon was the social centre of Baden-Baden, in the nineteenth century a cultural suburb of Paris. Hector Berlioz's *Béatrice et Bénédict* was first performed there in 1862, in French. The spa town had a casino that attracted the Prince of Wales and Russian aristocrats as well as Dostoevsky, who lost his last rouble there—hence his novel *The Gambler.*

Having made an impression on high society, my grandfather had the confidence to open a jewellery boutique near the casino. It was to be open only during the social season in the summer. The boutique still flourished in Nazi Germany, thirty-five years after his death in 1902.

Now, in the spring of 1937, it was overwhelmingly evident that we were witnessing the disintegration of our world. The days of our ownership of the jewellery firm were numbered. Either we would have to find somebody to buy it or it would be seized. Our mother knew she had to leave but had no idea when or how. Margo and her husband, Paul, were in Cologne, preparing their emigration.

I was very conscious of being extraordinarily lucky to be able to go to Cambridge in the fall. Few others were that fortunate. I knew what I was going to do in the next three years. By 1937 few people still thought the Nazis were a passing phenomenon, that somehow they would go away. That had been the wishful thinking of many in the first three years. But even many of those who had no illusions about the seriousness of Nazi intentions found it difficult to decide to emigrate, for any number of reasons, hoping against hope that somehow they could remain relatively safe. No one predicted the Holocaust. That was beyond anybody's capacity to imagine.

I was never a candidate for immigration to Palestine. My future was in England. But my brother Robert, no doubt influenced by Emil Netter, played with that idea for a few months before deciding to go to America. As to other people, much of the talk I heard in Frankfurt was about visits to the English consulate, about quota numbers for American visas, and about applications for other visas to Cuba, the Dominican Republic, Turkey. Two cousins went to Palestine, and one to the United States. One of my father's cousins, Richard Koch, went to the Soviet Union with his wife and two of their five children. A doctor, Richard had been invited to run a sanatorium in Yessentuki in the Caucasus. He was entirely unpolitical and knew no Russian. When the Germans came in 1941, he had to flee. Before he was able to return, he wrote his memoirs, parts of which were published in Germany in 2003 under the title *Zeit vor Eurer Zeit. Autobiographische Aufzeichnungen. Medizin und Philosophie* (*A Time Before Your Time: Autobiographical Notes about Medicine and Philosophy*). His son Friedrich fought in the Red Army and survived.

As for me, there was an enormous amount of thinking behind the idea of my going to Cambridge for three years. It was hoped that *somehow* a way could be found for the Koch jewellery firm to be transferred to Bond Street in London, to the rue de la Paix in Paris, or to Fifth Avenue in New York, and that I was the man to take it over. I certainly realized that the chance of this happening was almost zero. However, using magical thinking, the prospect could not be ruled out altogether. Sending me to Cambridge was to be the first step. Friends I would make there would buy my jewellery in the decades to come. What was wrong with that?

No, it could not be ruled out. I did not resist the idea but did not think much about it. On those occasions when I did, I told myself that I was genetically well conditioned to become a first-class jeweller, even though I had absolutely no experience. I could probably bluff my way to the top and do quite well. I liked the artistic challenge.

of designing beautiful things and the social challenge of persuading people to buy them. I never talked about this with the anti-imperialist socialist Pop, who probably had another future in mind for me. I did, however, mention it to Daria, who did not react one way or another.

My being groomed as a jeweller was primarily the idea of my cousin Rudolf Heilbrunn, the son of my father's sister, Claire, who had died in 1936.

Rudolf's father, Uncle Ludwig, was an eminent lawyer and had been a deputy in the *Landtag* before the First World War. He had played a prominent role in the creation of the University of Frankfurt and was an amateur Goethe scholar. He had a large law practice and was close to my mother. His office was in the Koch building near the Frankfurter Hof.

By temperament Rudolf was an academic. His interests were historical and philosophical, and he was an obsessive book buyer. His specialty was Spinoza. He had studied law at Heidelberg and would have become a professor or joined his father's law practice had he not had to yield to family pressure to become a partner at Robert Koch. But after my father's death in 1919, there were no other family members in line of succession.

Rudolf was not a natural jeweller, as our grandfather Robert Koch had been, or his younger brother Louis, who took over the firm after his death and ran it superbly with spectacular success—without any advertising—until his death in 1930. Uncle Louis was enormously persuasive, ingratiating, and enterprising. He was an enthusiastic collector of paintings, rings, and, above all, musical autographs. His collection included Schubert's song *Die Forelle* ("The Trout") and his last three piano sonatas, and letters by Mozart and Beethoven. Uncle Louis was also a generous philanthropist and a prominent member of the Jewish community.

Two weeks before Hitler came to power in 1933, Rudolf married Lore Grages. We all liked her immensely. She was a member of a prominent family and was not Jewish. It was the only mixed marriage in our immediate family. Robert and I recited verses at their wedding, composed by Uncle Ludwig. Now, four years later, Lore resisted the suggestion by some members of her family that having a Jewish husband at a time like this was not a good idea, whatever his charms, and that she should divorce him. She remained loyal to Rudolf.

It was universally known in Frankfurt that Robert Koch was a Jewish store. On the Nazi-organized national boycott day of April 1, 1933, a stormtrooper had been planted in front of the store—as other stormtroopers had been planted in front of other Jewish stores throughout Germany. However, in spite of Nazi threats, the store continued to do well under the management of Rudolf and his partners. Now, in 1938, it was up to him to manage the final phase, its sale to an "Aryan." The technical word for this "Aryanization" of the business world was *Arisierung*.

That summer, to give me a push in the direction in which he wanted me to go, Rudolf arranged for me to spend a few weeks in the jewellery store and observe how things were done. I did not object. I had nothing else to do.

I went to the store every day and sat in a corner and watched. The staff was nice to me but not very interested. Customers came in, were served, either bought something or did not. The only thing I learned was that at least two sales people had to be in the room if there was only one customer present, in case of trouble. There never was any trouble. I was bored to tears.

CHAPTER 6

1938: The Year I Met Daria

I WENT TO CAMBRIDGE IN THE FALL OF 1937. AMONG my fellow refugee students there was the enchanting Hilde Litthauer. I had a serious crush on her throughout my first term. She did not notice. Hilde studied economics, as did I. Whenever she missed a lecture, I lent her my notes, which she copied with appropriate gestures of gratitude. That was the only sentiment she displayed toward me. After the first year, she switched to psychology, as I did to law, and I rarely saw her again. After inflaming a number of others, she married the eminent virologist E.B. Himmelweit, originally from Berlin, and became the first professor of social psychology in the United Kingdom, founding the social psychology department at the London School of Economics and, in effect, establishing the discipline on the university curriculum. In 1957 she made her reputation as the author of *Television and the Child*, the first scholarly work on the subject in England or North America.

There was much joy in living in St. John's College, in one of the most beautiful university towns in the world. I put on cap and gown for dinner every evening "in Hall" in the shadow of a portrait of Lady Margaret Beaufort, who founded the college in 1511. I had a room at A4 Chapel Court. To have tea or sherry with friends in New Court, I had to cross the Bridge of Sighs over the river Cam.

Yes, there was much joy in living in Cambridge at that time but there was something unreal about it, a suspicion that this experience was actually meant for somebody else. But I cannot deny that I had a splendid time, even if in my first year I could not become excited about economics, which always seemed to be either obvious or incomprehensible. Music was more rewarding. I played second violin in a string quartet and, in my second year, in the orchestra of *The Marriage of Figaro* in the Arts Theatre—an exhilarating experience, even though, being placed below the stage, I never saw the opera.

At the end of my first academic year, in the spring of 1938, I went back to Frankfurt, not sure what I was going to do during the summer. My mother was determined to leave as soon as she could, probably for England, perhaps together with Uncle Ludwig. But she still did not know when. She was delaying her decision to emigrate because, among other things, she was also trying to arrange her mother's emigration. Rudolf was in Lausanne, Switzerland, which, in his view, was the right place from which to negotiate the Aryanization of Robert Koch. Lore was in Holland, preparing the ground for their change of domicile.

One evening my mother and I went to a concert of the Jüdische Kulturbund, the Jewish cultural federation, at our synagogue, the Westend Synagogue, within walking distance of the Westendplatz. Beginning in 1933, Jewish artists, writers, musicians, actors, and all others engaged in cultural activities had been gradually dismissed from public institutions and instructed to serve only Jewish audiences and deal primarily with Jewish subject matter. Increasingly the Kulturbund assumed enormous importance in the shrinking Jewish world. The line between Jewish and non-Jewish audiences was relatively easy to draw, but to differentiate German from Jewish art was considerably more difficult. The SS officer Hans Hinkel, whom Goebbels had appointed to administer the program, and the Jewish leaders with whom he was supposed to work were rarely on the same wavelength. One heard many stories about their relationship. Their meetings were described as reasonably civil, certainly at first. They agreed that Mendelssohn was incontrovertibly of Jewish descent and his works were therefore allowed, never mind that he composed the *Reformation Symphony* in 1830 to mark the three hundredth anniversary of the Presentation of the Augsburg Confession, a key document of Lutheranism. On the other hand, Hinkel had a problem with Handel, the composer of the oratorios *Solomon*, *Esther*, *Deborah* and *Saul*. In Hinkel's mind Handel, presumably a pure Aryan, was profoundly misguided when he spent so much of his time and energy on undeniably Jewish subjects. At first Hinkel was lenient, but by the spring of 1937 Handel, Bach, Beethoven and Brahms were no longer allowed, whatever the subject matter. By the end of that year, Schumann was also *verboten*, followed by Mozart and Schubert in the spring of 1938.

By 1938 it had also become difficult to gather the necessary talent for a full orchestra. There was especially a shortage of brass players, which, for example, made it hard to perform any symphony of Mahler later than the first. Some of the early Kulturbund celebrities, the conductor Hans Wilhelm Steinberg for one, had been lured to the Palestine Symphony, founded by Arturo Toscanini and Bronislaw Huberman, and so had a number of other musicians. But it was remarkable that in Frankfurt, and elsewhere, despite ever diminishing resources, the standard of performance remained admirably high.

The evening my mother and I went to the Westend Synagogue, Tchaikovsky's *Fifth Symphony* was on the program. There was no problem with Tchaikovsky—he was Slav. Miraculously, enough brass players had emerged. During the first few bars of the second movement, I suddenly bent over with a violent pain in my abdomen. It was as though I had been pierced by a needle. My mother, correctly assuming that I was having an attack of appendicitis, led me out of the synagogue. She took a taxi home and phoned Dr. Viktor Schmieden, our family surgeon and, although she did not know it, special medical adviser to the *Reichswehr* and the *Wehrmacht*. Dr. Schmieden, of course, knew we were Jewish. He demanded that she take me to his hospital immediately—the municipal hospital, not the Jewish hospital. I was admitted—no questions asked—even though Jewish patients were no longer allowed in non-Jewish hospitals. I was to be operated on first thing in the morning, to prevent perforation. As Dr. Schmieden's patient, I was treated with respect and civility throughout my stay there.

Just before the anaesthetist put a mask on my face to make me inhale the ether, Dr. Schmieden came in. I was still awake. The last sound I heard was his greeting to his staff: "Heil Hitler."

I was told later, but cannot corroborate, that in the 1920s Josef Mengele had been one of his interns.

To recover from the surgery, my mother took me to Zürich, to a cheap hotel very different from the luxury hotels in which we used to stay in better times. She spent a few days with me and then went back home. A few months later, when we were again in Switzerland together, the dilemma of whether or not to return to Frankfurt was agonizing. But not this time. She did not yet feel in any acute personal danger, and I did not try to influence her. The main purpose of her trip was to accompany me.

In March, Hitler had annexed Austria. His next target was Czechoslovakia. He demanded that German-speaking Sudetenland, an integral part of the country, join Germany. Czechoslovakia had an alliance with France. The British had a moral obligation to protect it. Neville Chamberlain was prime minister. Both Britain and France wanted to avoid war at almost any cost. Ribbentrop, now Hitler's foreign minister, had been ambassador in London and had been a welcome weekend guest in the mansions of the Clivedon Set, aristocrats sympathetic to the anti-Bolshevik Nazi cause. Now, it was assumed, he told Hitler the British would cave in. The Swiss papers were well informed.

Few of the refugees I saw in Zürich thought there was a chance to avoid war. But one always hoped for a miracle. As far as I was concerned, the important thing was that my mother, Margo, and Paul got out of Germany in time.

I saw Rudolf in Lausanne. He was too intelligent to be an optimist. However, ever since he had had a bout of meningitis when he was twenty, he went through occasional episodes of euphoria, the symptom of which usually was a spree of frantic book buying. This time the symptom was different: he told me to keep my eyes on the generals.

There had been stories in the Swiss papers about dissent in the general staff. General Ludwig Beck, chief of staff of the German Army in particular, was said to be opposed to Hitler's military leadership. Rudolf thought there was a good chance he would lead a coup. Despite his euphoria, this was by no means far-fetched.

I had great respect for Rudolf and liked him a lot. But he was not always right. Leaving aside his euphoric phases, I remembered that in June 1934, four years earlier, during the bloody Röhm putsch, he said, sitting with us on the veranda of our grandmother's house in Kronberg, "This is the Battle of the Marne of the Nazis," meaning the turning point. It was not.

Rudolf was pleased to see me. He wanted me to tell him all about Cambridge and thought it was a good idea for me to switch from economics to law. He told me about his negotiations with the famous Robert Bosch company in Stuttgart who were interested in buying our store and the boutique in Baden-Baden—including the valuable building in Frankfurt designed by Paul Wallot, the architect of the Reichstag in Berlin, at its prime location at the corner of the Kaiserstrasse and the Neue Mainzerstrasse. Contact had been established through an intermediary in London. But, of course, we would receive only a fraction of the real value and none of the proceeds could be taken out of Germany. The name Robert Koch would remain attached to the business. The talks were conducted in a professional, not unfriendly manner. This appeared to be the best solution for us under the circumstances. The sale would go through.

In the meantime, Rudolf thought it might be a good idea for me to learn something about pearls. There was no need for me to go back to Cambridge until early October. Would I agree to spend September in Antwerp?

September 11, 1938
Antwerp! The name draws tears down my hoary cheeks. It is connected with my first experience of "furrin" parts. I was nine and Michal eleven, and we went to Belgium with our French governess. At Harwich, it being late, we were pushed onto a boat and stuffed into bunks. "*Mes enfants,*" cried Mademoiselle tragically, appearing from nowhere in a nightdress, "*il faut s'habiller, nous sommes au Hook of Holland.*" However, in the end we struggled onto another boat, the right one, and there was a horrific storm, and we watched with interest while Mademoiselle was very sick, owing, as she afterwards explained, to a bad cup of tea. When we eventually arrived in Antwerp, we were not allowed to breakfast in the first class restaurant as it had been

reserved for the Prince of Wales. I always remember this. It made me very indignant at the time, I considering myself far superior to any prince, and caused the birth of my conversion to Socialism. Mademoiselle's aunt met us at the station, wearing gloves and smelling faintly of lavender. We nicknamed her *la petite grosse* and were overcome with shame and embarrassment because she discovered this. I think she has now gone the way of all flesh, but hope perhaps I may be mistaken.

Rudolf spoke to his business friend Rappaport, who would be pleased to give me a month's course. I thought that might be an interesting experience and said yes. It could never do me any harm to learn something new. I undertook to get in touch with Monsieur Rappaport and give him my telephone number. For the next few days I would find an agreeable spot, not too far from Lausanne, to await further developments. After that, I would go to a place near Antwerp, to be on call.

I had heard good things about Champéry only an hour away from Lausanne, near the French border. A travel bureau suggested the Hotel Mirabeau. That was where Daria was staying.

CHAPTER 7

Daria's First Letters

Champéry, August 10, 1938

I am starting this letter without ceremony or prefix, as I really have no idea what to call you and anyhow always find it much easier to address nothing other than a name. In your letter to me, supposing, which is only right and proper, that you should feel inclined to write to me, you may indicate your wishes in this matter.

I have been obliged to answer many exceedingly embarrassing questions with regard to your conduct and person. Knowing your unaccountable curiosity on the score, I will try to retail all that has been asked of me.

Mrs. Wharry, irritable but with an amiable smile: "Really you must not do such things. Of course I know the young man is perfectly respectable (?), but what will people think of you?" Angela: "Now you really have started a scandal, old bean, roaring into the hotel at all hours of the night." Bea, of course: "What did you talk about, where did you go? Did he kiss you? Who are his parents? Has he any money?" The members of the Dutch family, with the exception of the father who had no interest in such things, were all very insinuating, but I stared them firmly in the eye and the prosecution collapsed. Mary Bigweather, she with whom I am but frigidly acquainted if indeed at all, rushed into the office yesterday afternoon and emerged brandishing a letter: "For you from Chamonix!" she screamed, in the shrill falsetto of one who is about to reveal a thrilling intrigue to the whole world and finds her wonted voice inadequate for the purpose. It was, however, a note from my closest friend informing me that someone whom I liked and respected and whom my friend admired enormously, and who was excessively kind to me in former years, had just been killed in the Spanish war. I feverishly hunted up an old paper to verify this and found that he, Lewis Clive by name, and another young man, a great friend of my elder sister, whom I remember fairly well, both died on the same day fighting for the same cause. What waste, what a waste, what a vile waste! No doubt all exceptionally nice people get killed early in this world by the nasty ones, as they are in the majority. A precocious little girl once answered to a fatuous old woman in my presence, "Yes, I am very good, but I try not to be too good, because if you are people hate you."

The family Wharry, and others, think I am brooding over your absence, and as this gives them pleasure and I have no intention of affording them an opportunity to sentimentalise, I am obliged to indulge this belief. Most galling, I feel, that the hitherto unpolluted name of Hambourg has been sullied and dragged in the dust.

I was in Knokke, the Belgian seaside resort not far from the Dutch border, when that letter arrived. What a delightful new friend I had acquired! Obviously she loved writing letters and did it well. And what role-playing talent—putting herself in the role of Juliet writing to her Romeo. I found that very amusing. I said so in my reply. And repeated it in a subsequent letter. To which I got an immediate answer:

Champéry, August 15
Angela and Bea are thrilled by the munificence of the postman. Please send your communications less

obviously. They seem to arrive without exception at mealtimes and are handed to me very publicly by the maid with the hors d'oeuvres.

You may find scandal amusing but I am galled by it. Just as much, inexplicably, on your behalf as on my own.

I did not give that scandal a moment's thought. I was much more interested in Daria's account of her stay in Paris where she visited her older sister Sonia and was entertained by her boss, the editor of Albatross Press, and his wife.

London, August 27
I arrived in Paris late at night and made what I fondly hoped was a most elegant and correct impression on my host and hostess. Later in the privacy of the bathroom, I discovered that the effect must have been a little marred by the fact that my face was pitch-black and I had torn a large hole in the most conspicuous part of my stocking. The Albatross Press inhabits a most befittingly celestial house with a courtyard: one side overlooks Notre Dame and the other overlooks the Seine. My bedroom on a terrace was just above the one-time meeting place of Eloise and Abelard. You, with your habitual

independence and general superiority, cannot imagine how delightful it was to be allowed to explore, or rather partly explore, Paris unescorted. I sauntered nonchalantly down the banks of the Seine, picking at the book stalls and the print stalls and all other stalls, and savouring the people, and afterwards drifted into Notre Dame, where I looked at all the wrong things and ended up by hitting my hand with tremendous violence on the Gros Bourdon. I am still preserving the bruise.

A terrific intellectual dinner party took place during my visit, under the strain of which my intelligence shrank back abashed, and finally sank altogether. This only proves, as I had always suspected, that I am cleverer than other people think me but not nearly as clever as I think myself. A young man, at least not very young, accosted me with the remark, "I love peasants, but the English ones are so unapproachable, don't you think?" At first I imagined that he was thinking about birds and prepared for a most interesting and cheerful discussion, but then I discovered that he alluded to people, flesh and blood, human beings so to speak. I relapsed heavily into silence. To some other great brain, I unfortunately and presumptuously asserted that I hoped to become a writer. "Ah," said he, "now tell me, are you interested in individuals or the mass? Do you take a type to represent a multitude? That is much deeper I think." I agreed that it was infinitely deeper and hastily fled from him. I then sat, feeling unpleasantly young and stupid and inexperienced, in an armchair and listened to the intelligent conversation. As the hours and the words flew on, I had an extraordinary sensation of growing younger and younger, passing backwards through childhood and infancy, until I finally became a baby in my nurse's arms. After that I went to bed with all possible speed.

CHAPTER 8

Waiting for Monsieur Rappaport

ON AUGUST 11, WITH DARIA'S VOICE STILL ECHOING
in my ears, I checked into the one-star Hotel St. Moritz in
Knokke, conveniently situated in a side street three blocks
from the promenade. It was good enough. I notified Monsieur Rappaport's office and phoned my mother. To Daria
I sent a postcard with my address.

This was the first summer since I had left Frankfurt in
1935 when I had to decide for myself what to do for my holidays, as it was no longer possible to cross the German border
without running the risk of arrest. I noticed in the paper on
the day I arrived that in Germany all male Jews had to add
the name *Israel* to their identification papers, and female
Jews the name *Sara*. How could anybody take that seriously?

Soon after my arrival I met a beautiful girl from Dort-
mund. She was two years older than I and had long black
hair and light blue eyes and smelled deliciously of lavender

soap. I felt no disloyalty toward Daria, who I thought was too young for me. I did not consider her a girlfriend but a delightful new friend, period. The Romeo and Juliet role-playing was her invention, not mine. One day after lunch, while her parents were having their siesta, the lavender girl—I have forgotten her name—lifted the barrier between the spheres of children and grown-ups by introducing me gently to the joys of sex. It was marvelous. I had been hoping for some time for such a transformative event. This was the perfect moment. It was lovely being grown-up.

The lavender girl told me afterward, while we were both enjoying a post-coital, very grown-up cigarette, that she and her parents preferred to go abroad for their summer holidays because the German resorts were full of Nazis. That was rather a daring thing to say to someone she had just met, whatever the circumstances. All I had told her about myself was that I was a student in England. She did not ask me why. She said her boyfriend was in the army and thought the Nazis were going to provoke the West quite soon and Stalin would not mind at all. Did I think the English were ready to fight? I did not really think so, I said, but there were a lot of people in England who were slowly waking up. It was not easy for them because it was, after all, only twenty years after the last war. She said her father knew the English quite well and was appalled two years before when Ribbentrop, when he had become ambassador, gave the Nazi salute to the king. That should have made them sit up, she said.

I do not know whether it was as a result of my conversations with Daria, with whom I had not spoken directly about the danger of war, or the result of the things the lavender girl said, that I began to become—most uncomfortably—aware of the immorality of my position: I was actually hoping for a war.

I was born in 1919, the year after the Great War ended. I vividly remembered the men with one or more of their limbs missing, begging in the streets, still wearing uniforms, victims of the war. Two uncles of mine had been killed in the last year of the war, the brothers of my mother and my father, and I knew that the fathers of some of my school friends, men who had been in the trenches, were unable to speak about their experiences. I recalled that my grandmother Kahn's house, the house in which my mother and her brothers had grown up, had been a *Lazarett*, a hospital for the wounded. And I also remembered from my early childhood a picture book of the Franco-Prussian War of 1870–71, a book with coloured pictures of dying men and horses on a blood-soaked battlefield. It had made a pacifist of me for life. The war memorial near my grandmother Koch's house in Kronberg told me in Latin, *dulce est pro patria mori*—it is sweet to die for one's fatherland. I could not believe such a thing.

And now here I was, hoping for another war. Did I know what I was doing? Was a war the only way to get rid of the Nazis? I realized Rudolf was hoping for a generals' putsch. There were stories in the papers suggesting that Rudolf may have been right and that something along those lines was actually happening. Beware of wishful thinking, I told myself. The Nazis would know how to suppress any incipient revolt in the bud. Everyone knew that most generals approved of Hitler undoing the Versailles Treaty. I was sure that when the chips were down they would support him, even if they thought Hitler was too low-class for their tastes and resented that he was giving too much power to the SS and to the SA at their expense, and thought that in his speeches he often went too far and was playing with fire.

By now Germany was a police state. There were dozens of concentration camps. I had heard of people who had been in one and got out.

It was uncanny that the sun was always shining when Hitler made his moves. There was "Hitler weather" when he marched into the Rhineland in March 1936, when the Allies could easily have stopped him. That was when *he* was not ready to fight. The sun was shining when he took Austria in March. Providence, as he called it, was always on his side.

And here I was, hoping for Providence to be on our side.

As I was watching all the happy people on the beach—the children building castles in the sand, the lovely girls—I was thinking of the stories I had heard about the innocent summer of 1914, the last summer before the catastrophe that no one had anticipated. On the contrary, during that summer people were looking forward to a war as a kind of liberation. Was I hoping that this was another innocent pre-war summer?

On August 25 I received a phone call. I thought it was Monsieur Rappaport in Antwerp, telling me he was ready for me at last. But it was a stranger who gave his name—Dr. Grünberg—and said he was calling from Lausanne. He said he was a friend of Rudolf's, who did not want to call himself because he did not want to take the responsibility.

"The responsibility for what?"

"The responsibility for your returning to Frankfurt. I told your cousin this was a matter for you to decide, not for him. I asked him to give me your phone number and I would call you."

I asked him to explain.

"A man in uniform visited your mother and asked for you. It is true, isn't it, that you are still technically domiciled in Frankfurt?"

"I think so."

"Well, that is the reason. You were being called up to serve in the army. You were in the *Ersatzreserve Zwei*, Army

Reserve Number Two. When your mother said you were abroad, the man said you had better come home right away, or there would be consequences."

"Consequences? You mean consequences for my mother?"

"I don't see what else it could mean. Of course, she would not call you herself to tell you this."

I gave this ten seconds to sink in.

"Of course I will go right away," I said. "It was good of you to call. You did the right thing."

"Thank you. You see, there is no consistency about the way the Nazis interpret the Nuremberg laws. They don't say specifically that non-Aryans can't serve in the military. A number of them do. May I make a suggestion?"

"Please do."

"Don't cross the border by train. Fly. Much less risky. They don't look for whoever they are looking for on planes and in airports. They think people who can fly are by definition harmless."

I sent Daria another postcard telling her I had to leave Knokke for a few days.

I left things deliberately vague. It was therefore no surprise that she was thoroughly confused.

Late August 1938

Filled with alarm, indignation and apprehension, I am writing you this which is not a letter but a communication.

Must you return to the wasps' nest?

I know, of course, that you are too proud, but I feel quite confident that I could manage to raise up enough money, my own and others', to enable you to conduct things safely.

Otherwise, I have written to my aunt, Lady Clive, British Embassy, Brussels, wife of the British ambassador, prognosticating your appearance and instructing to provide consuls and other necessities. Her attitude towards young people differs from that of my parents, apart from which she is enlightened, kind, witty at times, and the friend of my friends. Do not fear or hesitate to accost her. You need not, of course.

Are you in Belgium? I should be very happy to assist you, if necessary, and at the risk of offending your proud spirit, by writing to my uncle in Brussels, the British Ambassador Sir Robert Clive, or my ancient governess in Gilly, Charleroi. You need not thank me for this never-to-be-realised offer as I love being officious and the very fact of making it gives me an unjustifiable feeling of prestige.

CHAPTER 9

Fifteen Minutes with the Police

I TOOK THE PLANE FROM BRUSSELS TO COLOGNE. IT was my first experience in an airplane—another first experience as an adult. But it was considerably less memorable than my time with the lavender girl. In fact, the one thing I remember vividly was that no one noticed the "Israel" missing from my passport. There was nothing in my papers to suggest that I fell on the wrong side of the Nuremberg laws. Officialdom saw no reason to ask me any unnecessary questions, such as "Why aren't you in uniform?"

August 30, 1938
PLEASE, please, please kindly explain to me in detail exactly what it feels like to fly. Personally, I nourish the most bigoted and unshakeable conviction about it, as, having flown with my own wings in dreams (this is not intentionally sentimental), I am

determined never to fly with any others—that is to say, never at all. Of course, of course, it is ridiculous. I openly acknowledge the fact. I do not trust myself entirely to the sovereign guidance of reason, as I have found, and expect to find, that though an excellent and useful thing in its way, the uses of reason are limited, and there are times when it is superfluous, times when it is futile, and times when it fails altogether! Very bold of me to say so to you, I think. I expect to be overwhelmed by a storm of protestations and indisputable logic.

I phoned my sister Margo from the Cologne airport. She was amazed to hear my voice. I had not notified her I was coming. We had not spoken since the spring when she visited me in the hospital after my surgery. I was not worried about anybody listening in. After all, I was law abiding: I was doing what the authorities wanted me to do. I was going to Frankfurt to terminate my domicile there. The technical word was *abmelden*—to deregister.

I told Margo I was going to take the afternoon train to Frankfurt.

"Good," she said. "Then there will be time for you to have lunch with us. Paul will be pleased to see you. We'll take you to the station afterward."

Margo was seven years older than I; Paul, eight years.
We always got on well. After inquiring whether I had heard
from Monsieur Rappaport in Antwerp—I admitted I was
rather pleased that I had not—they asked me, as they usually did, about my love life.

They knew about Hilde Litthauer, the economics student who had shown an inexplicable preference for other
admirers.

"Is there nobody else?" Paul asked.

It did not occur to me to mention the lavender girl.
In any case, she would have left by the time I returned to
Knokke, and I never asked for her address. I felt no need
to see her again.

"I met a very nice English girl two weeks ago in
Champéry. She writes beautifully. I'm sure she's going to
be a great writer—she's only seventeen—I like her a lot.
At the moment she is definitely too young for me, but I
think—for some reason I can't explain—that she will never
be my girlfriend."

"Don't say never," Paul said. "One never knows."

Margo smiled, and changed the subject. Soon it was
time to leave for the station. On the train to Frankfurt
I began to get nervous about my visit to the police but
decided to think about other things.

To say that my mother was pleased to see me would
be a gross understatement. That uniformed visitor had

been very upsetting to her. She had my phone number in Knokke but would not use it to ask me to come. She, too, had heard stories about boys in my situation being picked up at the border. One solution that occurred to her was simply to take flight and leave. She had a valid passport. The Nazis wanted Jews to emigrate—they never seized passports. She could go to Switzerland. Lilli Wollstein, a school friend of hers who lived in Ascona in the Italian part of Switzerland near Locarno, had asked my mother many times to visit her. But under the current circumstances, taking flight seemed risky to her. Suppose the uniformed visitor appeared again, found only the maid and the cook in the apartment, and rang the alarm bells. There could be all kinds of unpleasant consequences. They could confiscate everything she had and block her bank account. It was unnecessary to take that risk. There was a good chance she could emigrate legally. She had applied for English and American visas and was waiting for her number to come up. Most of her belongings could be shipped abroad.

But she was reluctant to leave her mother behind without being able to make firm plans for her emigration as well. Moreover, she hoped she could coordinate her departure to England with her brother-in-law, Uncle Ludwig, who could leave with her. Leaving legally, of course, meant paying the confiscatory *Reichsfluchtsteuer*—the Reich's flight tax, which meant, among other things, the surrender of her considerable collection of jewellery. That was still better than taking flight and losing everything.

I was afraid that I would find my mother in terrible condition and was relieved to find her coping reasonably well with the immense difficulties she was facing. In fact, as soon as I arrived, she suggested that if all went well she would like to spend a few days with me in Ascona. What did I think of that?

"An excellent idea," I said.

In the meantime, I was, to put it mildly, not looking forward to going to the police. The *Polizeipräsidium*—police headquarters—was a gigantic building opposite my old school, the Goethe Gymnasium, on the Platz der Republik. It was very much of a presence throughout my school years, though I had never been inside.

I asked the man at the front desk what office was competent to deal with an *Abmeldung*—a change of domicile. I was given the room number, on the third floor, way down several corridors. Complicated, but I found it.

I did not have to wait. The policeman in charge had little to do and my arrival seemed to be a pleasant change for him. There was a photograph of the *Führer* on the wall.

I told him what I wanted.

"Please be patient for a minute." He left the room and five minutes later came back with a dossier. My name was written on it together with a big, conspicuous, inescapable J—which could only mean one thing, *Jude,* Jew.

He opened the file and glanced at the top paper.

"So you don't want to serve in our army, Herr Koch?" he asked me.

I swallowed hard. "Well," I began, "you see—"

He cut me off.

"No need to go on. How long are you staying in Frankfurt?"

"Two days."

"And where are you going after that?"

"To Switzerland, with my mother."

He stamped a document with a loud noise.

"*Sie habe Schwein,*" he said, in vernacular Frankfurt German. You have pig—pig as in a piggybank. Translation: Some people have all the luck.

"*Gute Reise,*" he wished me as I left his office.

Elation is the best word I can think of to describe our mood that evening, the last evening I spent in Frankfurt with my mother before we departed for Switzerland. I did not return until three years after the war.

CHAPTER 10

Anguish in Ascona

Early September 1939
What a relief, o' what a relief, that you have emerged
from Germany. Let us now hope that all your trou-
bles are ended. If they are not I confidently assert
that it is better to be dogged by ill luck for the first
twenty-five years of one's life and to enjoy good
fortune ever afterwards, than vice versa.

My mother and I took the night train from Frankfurt.
When we woke up we were near the Swiss border. My
mother had been in Ascona before. I had not. I knew it was
a popular place for intellectual refugees. A few of them were
rich, but most of them were poor. I had heard a number of
eminent people had villas there. Emil Ludwig, the best-sell-
ing writer, was one. On the Monte Verità, the Mountain
of Truth, there was a fashionable hotel, originally a private

residence built by a famous architect in the Bauhaus style, on the site of an avant-garde "colony" where a few years earlier famous celebrities had gathered—Carl Gustav Jung, Isadora Duncan, Erich Maria Remarque, who had written *All Quiet on the Western Front*, and many others.

My mother stayed with her friend Lilli and her husband, Franz, in a lovely modern villa, halfway up the mountain, with a perfect view of the lake. I had known Tante Lilli all my life, but I preferred to stay downtown at the Hotel Ascona, even though the cuisine was superb in the Wollstein ménage. I hoped to meet some young people who were less fixated on their anxieties than their elders.

The butler, who was also the chauffeur, drove my mother down the mountain every day to join me. A few times he drove us to nearby Locarno.

Tante Lilli strongly urged my mother not to return to Frankfurt and to stay with her until the English or the Americans were ready to give her a visa. She put up every conceivable argument, with great eloquence, to make this plausible. Franz, she said, had good connections in Bern and could take care of all the formalities. This offer put my mother into a most agonizing quandary.

She could not sleep. Her anguish was made worse by our visits to the café on the main street of the ancient town, the meeting place of doom-saying refugees. Among them was a professor from Frankfurt whom she knew and who had a rich American wife and who was now writing a book. There was also a journalist from Zürich. They were both well informed on conditions in the concentration camps. So were a few other people we spoke to. The talk in Ascona was about the continuing Nazi pressure on Czechoslovakia, the real possibility of war, and the lack of preparedness of the Western democracies to face Hitler. What would Stalin do? And what about Mussolini? There was special scorn for British Prime Minister Neville Chamberlain and his fellow appeasers, who seemed to be calling the tune in London.

On the pleasant side, to compensate me for all that gloom and doom, there was an attractive Dutch girl who paid no attention to me and a beautiful girl called Gerda Levinson, who had written a novel about Palestine. She was more receptive to my attentions than the Dutch girl. I mentioned the two in a letter to Daria. For Gerda, Palestine was the place go to, especially if one was an idealistic young person eager to build a new society in the desert. "Making the desert bloom" was the common expression she also used.

September 11, 1938
I am grateful to you for describing, not always consciously, your attitude towards and progress with the female species, as I had long wanted to discover the reactions of men to women. Your Dutch friends

should have been singularly fortunate as, from slight but useful experience, I gather that most girls are anxious to "catch" boys no less than boys—I here rely on your evidence—are anxious to "catch" them. The extraordinary illusion appears to be, that when caught both parties consider themselves, and not the other, successful. It maketh me to marvel equally at the quaint conceit of man and the great cunning of Providence.

In the café, the refugees competed with each other in telling blood-curdling stories. A Swiss journalist told us that certain influential members of the English aristocracy were close to Hitler. After the Nazis had defeated the French, they would see to it that England would join the Nazis in a crusade against Bolshevik Russia. After all, in England the aristocracy was still in charge. The Duke of Windsor and his dreadful American wife were hoping to play a prominent role in the Nazi empire that was now unfolding, step by step. The dark ages were upon us.

In the end, Tante Lilli and Franz had to surrender. Their chauffeur took us to the station. My mother returned to Frankfurt, and I proceeded back to Knokke—by train via Paris, prepared, without enthusiasm, for Monsieur Rappaport to call.

He never called.

CHAPTER 11

"Peace in Our Time"

IN MARCH 1938 HITLER ANNEXED AUSTRIA. IN MAY
he demanded that Czechoslovakia cede the German-speaking Sudetenland, threatening military action. For the first
time since 1918, war seemed a real possibility. The tension
mounted. In August the German press was full of stories
about Czech atrocities against Sudeten Germans. The French
and the British coordinated their responses. Chamberlain had
some sympathy for the Sudeten Germans' right of self-deter-
mination. On September 15 Chamberlain visited Hitler on
his mountaintop near Berchtesgaden. For three hours they
talked. Three days later, Benito Mussolini made a speech
hinting he was on Hitler's side. On September 21 Hitler
demanded that the claims of ethnic Germans in Poland
and Hungary also be respected. On September 22 and 23
Chamberlain went to see Hitler again, this time in Godesberg near Cologne. At one stage Hitler told him that he

wanted Czechoslovakia to be completely dissolved and its territories redistributed to Germany, Poland, and Hungary, saying Chamberlain could take it or leave it. On September 24 Hitler issued the Godesberg Memorandum, which demanded that Czechoslovakia cede the Sudetenland to Germany no later than September 28. On September 26 Chamberlain sent Sir Horace Wilson to carry a personal letter to Hitler declaring that the Allies wanted a peaceful resolution to the Sudeten crisis. Later that evening, Hitler gave his reply in a speech at the Sportpalast in Berlin, in which he said Czechoslovakia must cede the Sudetenland to Germany or face war. On September 30 Chamberlain, his French counterpart Édouard Daladier, Mussolini, and Hitler gathered in Munich and signed an agreement that gave Germany the Sudetenland as of October 10. Hitler promised to go no further. The Czechs had no alternative but to capitulate. Stalin played no role in the proceedings. On September 30, after some rest, Chamberlain went to Hitler and asked him to sign a peace treaty between the United Kingdom and Germany. After Hitler's interpreter translated it for him, he happily agreed. On his return home Chamberlain announced that he had achieved "peace in our time."

September 11, 1938
I fear there will be a war and we must stomach it.

Europe is like a mind diseased, and as you know there is no cure for such an affliction, so perhaps it is as well for it to be destroyed after all.

Let us drink to a happier existence! I believe in one in spite of my convictions.

By the time the Munich Agreement was signed I was back in England. I cannot deny that I shared the universal relief, even though I knew better. I could always tell myself that when dealing with the future there were no certainties. Probabilities, yes, but no certainties.

The digs I rented for my second year in Cambridge at 2 Richmond Terrace, near the Round Church, were not yet ready. My pleasant landlady's name was Mrs. Ridley.

While waiting to move in, I stayed at the Premier Hotel, Russell Square, WC 1, for a few days. I gave Daria the address in a postcard. Neither of us suggested a meeting. She sent me this message:

"Promise me solemnly," I said to her as she lay on what I believed to be her death bed, "if you find in the world beyond the grave that you can communicate with me, that there is some way in which you can make me aware of your continued existence, promise me solemnly that you will not avail yourself

of it." She recovered, and never, never forgave me—
Samuel Butler

P.S. Could not resist this possible waste of a 1d
stamp.

On October 3 I took the train from Waterloo to Wey-
bridge in Surrey to see Max Morel, the father of my former
classmate Werner, who was not there. Max was a banker
from Frankfurt who had managed to transfer his business
to the City of London. He had always been close to my
family, particularly to Emil Netter.

He was in a terrible mood, so sick about the Munich
Agreement that he could not talk about it. But what he
did want to talk about—at great length and with a sharply
raised voice—was my gross misconduct. I had been shame-
lessly irresponsible, he shouted, to allow my mother to go
back to Frankfurt after leaving Ascona. I was now grown
up and should behave like a grown-up. He cut me short
when I replied that I would not presume to tell my mother
what to do—she had made all her own decisions since my
father's death in 1919. And the decision to go back had
been made after careful calculation of the risks involved
and been particularly painful for her. He would not listen
to me. I felt like an idiot for having so unnecessarily sub-
jected myself to his brutal harangue.

The first person I talked to once I was back in Cambridge was my friend George L. Mosse. He was studying English history, specializing in the Tudor period. The scion of a big Berlin publishing family, in later life he made a name for himself in the United States as a historian of German nationalism. Among the many books he wrote was one about the psychology—or rather the pathology—of German war memorials. The previous year I had spent a few days in Paris with George and his father and stepmother. It had been like being in the company of a dethroned monarch in exile.

I visited George in his modest digs near the station. Between us there was harmony, and seeing him restored my spirits. Thanks to the Munich Agreement, followed by my visit to Max Morel, though, I had a severe stomach ache.

His landlady was less civilized than Mrs. Ridley. She stood outside the lavatory door. When I came out she said, "Did you have to use all my lavatory paper?"

CHAPTER 12

Shattering Glass

Early December 1938
When one must attend lectures, make notes, read books and prepare for exams, it is not easy to deal with a life-and-death situation that stares one in the face but that one cannot control. It is tempting to put one's head in the sand. Obviously, that is not a rational policy. But what is? This was a question that kept me awake at night.

I did not find it easy to concentrate on the finer points of the laws of contract, tort, and real property when I heard the news on the BBC of the hair-raising happenings in Germany on November 9. I had to wait two interminable days before I was finally reassured by phone that my mother and Margo and Paul were safe.

The excuse for the pogrom—the burning of hundreds of synagogues throughout Germany and Austria, and the mass arrest of Jews, events now generally considered the beginning of the Holocaust—was the killing of a minor official at the German embassy in Paris. The killer was seventeen-year-old Herschel Grynszpan, who was living in Paris and made frantic by the arrest of his parents—together with thousands of other Polish Jews, who were deported from Germany to Poland but not permitted to enter by the Polish government. They were stuck at the border and were in despair. Grynszpan had wanted to shoot the German ambassador but he was not there. In his stead the young man killed a minor official by the name of Ernst vom Rath.

That was a name I recognized. The vom Rath family had a house down the street from my grandmother Koch in Kronberg. There was a second connection. My mother bought an Italian violin for me made in 1747 that had belonged to the vom Rath family. Money could not be taken out of the country, but violins could. It is insignificant details like these that stick in the mind.

In Cologne, when Margo and Paul heard stories of what was happening, they jumped into their car and drove south to Frankfurt, out of danger. Paul's father was an orthopaedic surgeon in Cologne. Nothing happened to him, this time. Three years later, however, when the Gestapo arrived to arrest him, he asked for a little delay because he had to look after his patients first. The delay was granted, but it made no difference: he and Paul's mother were deported to Theresienstadt in Czechoslovakia and did not survive.

In Frankfurt, as I heard later, they arrested Hans Erl, who sang bass roles in the opera and whom I had often heard perform. He had lost his job in 1933. The hundreds arrested during the night were taken to the city's *Festhalle*, the massive convention centre. At the entrance they had to give their names and professions to the Gestapo, after which they were ordered to sweep the floor.

"What is your name?" the Gestapo man asked Hans Erl.

He gave it to him.

"And profession?"

He told him.

"Really?" the man said. "Then sing something."

Erl gave this a moment's thought and then began to sing, in his hall-filling bass, Sarastro's aria from *The Magic Flute*:

In diesen heil'gen Hallen
Kennt man die Rache nicht.
Und ist ein Mensch gefallen,
Führt Liebe ihn zur Pflicht.
Dann wandelt er an Freundes Hand
Vergnügt und froh ins beßre Land.
Dann wandelt er an Freundes Hand
Vergnügt und froh ins beßre Land.

[In these holy halls
Revenge is not known.
And if a person strays,
Love will lead him back to duty.
Then, led by a friend's hand,
He wanders happily towards a better land].

When he finished, the man whispered to him, "You sang well. Now—run!"

Hans Erl did as he was told and returned home.

In 1942 he was arrested again, deported to Auschwitz, and sent to the gas chamber.

There is a memorial plaque in his honour at the Frankfurt Opera.

September 14, 1938
How vile, and narrow, and bigoted, and selfish, and petty, and intolerant, of anybody to care whether you are a Jew, a German, a negro, a half-caste or a Congo pigmy. Such people are not worth fraternizing with. At least you have the satisfaction of realizing inwardly that they ought to consider themselves honoured at having the opportunity of addressing you even a chance word. I cannot bear it, but in these enlightened times it seems impossible

to accept people for themselves and not for their denominations.

You do not speak to a Russian because you are conservative, or a German because you sympathize with Jews, or to a Jew because he is a black, or to an Indian because he is brown. Atheists refuse to hobnob with the even mildly religious-inclined, because religion to them must be inseparable from hypocrisy and ignorance. Socialists and conservatives are gradually becoming beings of a different order. They are as far apart as the inhabitants of Mars from those of Venus. They neither see with the same eyes, hear with the same ears, or speak with the same tongues, reason with the same brains, or feel with the same hearts. Each party is convinced that the other has neither eyes, ears, tongues, brains or hearts. I boil with rage at the mere contemplation of such stupidity.

CHAPTER 13

Christmas in Buckinghamshire

MY COLLEGE FRIEND JOHN GORRINGE INVITED ME
to spend my Christmas holidays at his home with his
mother and stepfather, Cecil H. Harper. The address was
Chesham Bois House, Amersham, Buckinghamshire. It was
the first and only time I experienced the English gentry.

One evening at dinner, Mr. Harper asked me what I
thought of the Nazis. I told him that thanks to them I considered war highly probable. He thought it strange that I
would speak so unkindly about my own country. Then he
asked me what I felt about Mr. Chamberlain. I replied that
I thought his approach was not likely to work.

He put down his napkin.

"So you want John to be killed in another war, do you?"
he asked and left the room.

I was tongue-tied and helpless, with a hollow feeling at
the pit of my stomach. I felt utterly alien.

The rest of my stay was entirely pleasant.

One year later, in early December 1939, I appeared before a recruiting board at St. John's College, Cambridge, and I declared my willingness to volunteer to serve in the army.

John reported this to his parents.

Mr. Harper wrote me this letter:

I would like to say how much I admire your courage and purpose in volunteering to join the Army. You have set an example to many of our young men who, in my opinion, are not over anxious to make the sacrifice you have so willingly made. But I can assure you that your action is appreciated and valued by all English men and women who would join with me in saying "Thank you." Perhaps in your spare odd moments you will find the time to let us know where and how you are.

I am afraid you will miss the quiet siesta after luncheon but there will be compensations.

My best wishes for your future and may it not be long before you are settling down again in that successful career.

Yours very sincerely,

Cecil H. Harper

CHAPTER 14

From Frankfurt to Kensington

AT LAST, *at last*, A MOMENTOUS EVENT OCCURRED: in early February of 1939—my mother arrived in London.

I had seen her last in September in Ascona. She had endured the ordeal of her legal emigration in reasonably good shape, even though she had to leave her mother behind, to follow later. She came with Uncle Ludwig. His son Rudolf had joined Lore in Holland.

Uncle Ludwig spoke very little English. Six years after the Nazis got into power he was still dumfounded by the inexplicable and unanticipated descent of Germany into barbarism. Now he was bewildered by his new surroundings.

My mother spoke English well, having been brought up by an English governess, Mim, whose name was Ethel Wilkins and who now lived in a retirement home in South

London. My mother was far more adaptable than her brother-in-law and adjusted quickly to the life of a refugee.

Very soon, Margo and Paul arrived from Cologne. None of the new arrivals had been allowed to take more than ten marks out of the country—and a minimum of luggage. They joined the others in a three-room flat in North End House in West Kensington, not far from Hammersmith. The flat was financed by the same funds that paid for my studies in Cambridge, a pre-Nazi account soon to be depleted. Nobody was allowed to work. To pay for my last year at Cambridge (1939–40), I had to borrow money from a bank.

Around the time Margo and Paul arrived, my mother picked up her eleven-year-old nephew Wolf Kahn at the station. He had come over with the *Kindertransport*, the rescue mission organized by the British government in conjunction with the Jewish community that took in nearly ten thousand children from Germany, Austria, and Czechoslovakia in the months before the war. I had been in touch with a refugee committee in Cambridge that undertook to look after Wolf. The first family to offer him a home happened to be headed by a professor of mine. Wolf never complained, but I soon noticed that the arrangement did not work at all. They had expected a poor, destitute child, and not a well-equipped, well-adjusted, cheerful little boy with a remarkable talent for drawing. Wolf later became a prominent New York painter, a favourite of Hillary Clinton. The committee found him another family, the father of which was a schoolteacher. It could not have worked out better. A year later, Wolf left England and joined the rest of his family in New York. Throughout the difficult postwar years, and thereafter, he regularly sent invaluable CARE parcels to the teacher and his family.

At the end of term in May, I squeezed into the flat in North End House and slept on a sofa. Uncle Ludwig spent much of his energy trying to learn English. He was stumped by an advertisement in the window of a funeral parlour in the Fulham Road, near Kensington High Street. It read: "A well-conducted funeral need not be expensive."

"Conduct?" he asked. "Who is the conductor?"

The *Times* kept him busy for hours every morning, especially the Court Gazette. One day he read that there was a garden party at Buckingham Palace. Among the invited was Ludwig Koch, a first cousin of his wife and my father, whose passion for animals was alien to my uncle. There had been a split in the Koch family, with the eccentric, imaginative and lovable Ludwig Koch on one side and the more conventional, prosaic Kochs, my side, on the other. The passion for animals had enabled Ludwig Koch to become famous for his pioneering recordings of birdsongs broadcast by the BBC. Part of the charm of those broadcasts was Ludwig Koch's pronounced Frankfurt accent.

"What country have we come to?" his namesake Uncle Ludwig Heilbrunn asked. "The King invites Ludwig Koch to a garden party at Buckingham Palace. I wouldn't have opened the door for him at my house."

CHAPTER 15

Watches and Clocks

MY MOTHER INDECISIVE? SOMETIMES, YES. BUT A FEW weeks after her arrival in England, we discovered that before emigrating she had made a decision that required extraordinary courage and involved grave risks. With the help of a heroically loyal and enterprising employee of Robert Koch, she smuggled my father's collection of 161 antique watches and clocks, some made as early as the sixteenth century, to Holland, and from there to England.

I was at school in England when she made that decision. But when I was in Frankfurt during my holidays, my mother never said a word about it, nor did she say anything during our time together in Ascona. It was not the kind of decision she would discuss with her children. The only person who was privy to it was her brother-in-law, Ludwig, who strongly advised against it, on the grounds that one should not put one's life in the hands of an employee. She ignored him. I have always been amazed that she had the strength to wrestle with this alone, only two years after she had been traumatized by the suicide of her second husband.

In my childhood, the collection was rarely mentioned. My father probably acquired it before the First World War at the suggestion of Uncle Louis. He was not really a collector, in the usual sense. His heart was in his horses.

The collection was housed in a baroque cupboard in the hall of our apartment and was shown to visitors only on rare occasions. When the cupboard doors opened, a light went on inside. For us children seeing the treasures was a rare but festive occasion. My favourite watch was an eighteenth-century tulip. To see the time, you had to pull down the petals.

The presence of these treasures on our premises was, in a sense, incongruous. My mother preferred austerity to luxury, and any display of wealth was anathema to her. Her mother, Anna Kahn, had been a small-town girl whose background had been genteel but impoverished. She had found it difficult to live up to the lifestyle expected of the wife of the prominent banker Bernhard Kahn. My mother, though much more worldly, was a little like her. I knew the presence of the glittering collection in her home, even hidden in a cupboard, made her uncomfortable, although I do not remember her ever saying so.

The display of wealth, however, was by no means incongruous for the Kochs. It was the bread and butter of court jewellers. When in 1911 my mother announced that she was engaged to the rich and glamorous Otto Koch, her father was by no means enchanted. To the Kahns the Kochs were nouveaux riches. The Kahns had become wealthy a generation earlier, which made all the difference.

It was remarkable, in fact, how quickly the Kochs had established their eminence. The jewellery firm had been founded in 1879. The firm had prospered in parallel with the spectacular upward curve of the new Germany, which had been united in 1871. Imperial and royal charters decorated the walls of the store. One hangs in my den as I write this. By the time of the death of its founder, my grandfather Robert Koch, in 1902, its clients included many of the princely families in Germany, among them the Kaiser, not to mention the royal family of Italy. Not only European royalty: One day around 1910 the King of Siam appeared with his entourage at the Koch boutique in Baden-Baden. With a golden baton, His Majesty's adjutant pointed to the necklaces, broaches, bracelets, and rings on exhibition. My father's younger brother Max was in charge. He did not at first understand that the gesture meant that the king had ordered his assistant to buy the jewels. Soon Max did understand, and the adjutant paid cash. Max phoned his uncle Louis in Frankfurt and told him that, thanks to the royal visit, they were sold out.

A sumptuously furnished room at the back of the Frankfurt store was called the *Kaiserzimmer*, allegedly reserved for the Kaiser. This was pure fantasy, or should I say pure PR. The Kaiser never came: he never visited Frankfurt, whose municipal government he despised. It was social democratic. My father allegedly went to Bad Homburg, north of the city, to see him. I remember a pencilled sketch of a tiara, said to have been drawn by His Majesty himself. It was probably just as much fantasy as the *Kaiserzimmer*. The room was used for favoured customers, even after 1918.

My mother was not brought up to make a decision that would involve risking her life by trusting an employee. But she did, and our gratitude to this man for spiriting the clock collection out of Germany is immeasurable. He seems to have had good relations with somebody in the Nazi Party. This helped him pull it off. I do not think my mother ever found out how he did it.

On June 20, 1939, the collection was sold at an auction at Christie's in London. It was identified in the catalogue as "The Property of a Lady." My mother's name was not mentioned. It yielded £2,175, a substantial sum at the time. A new Austin car could be bought for £122 and a detached three-bedroom bungalow with garage and garden for £350. The sale enabled my mother to live in reasonable comfort for several years thereafter. Her income was supplemented by modest earnings derived from various jobs she took in London during the war.

In 2011 I discovered that fourteen of the watches and clocks had found their way to the British Museum. Their researchers had established that they had belonged to a Mrs. Netter, who had sold them at an auction at Christie's in June 1939. Details were unknown.

I followed this up and learned that perhaps a court of law might rule that the auction had taken place "under duress." At first glance, this seemed rather far-fetched. Nobody forced my mother to sell the collection: she was a free agent, and there was no comparison between her situation and the situation of those who, in Germany and Nazi-occupied territories, had to leave their treasures behind when they were arrested and deported or were compelled to surrender them before emigrating. However, the advice I received was quite clear. I was told that in British law the concept of duress might cover a situation in which a person has been compelled by straitened circumstances to do something that normally would have been inconceivable. So I requested a ruling by the Spoliation Advisory Panel, a body established by the British Parliament to look into cases of this kind. The panel consisted of ten eminent legal and academic experts. After careful examination, in 2012 they found that indeed the auction was a forced sale under the circumstances, but that the price paid by Christie's in 1939 was fair. The duress was "at the lower end of the scale of gravity of such cases." The British Museum undertook to make it clear in its description of the exhibits that they had originated in the Koch-Netter collection. In an informal communication, the secretariat of the panel suggested we had done the right thing to put the case before the panel.

Everyone was satisfied.

If the duress had been on the upper end of the scale and a court of law had agreed, the auction would have been decreed invalid and we would still be the owners of the 161 watches and clocks, including my favourite tulip watch. By then however, they had been acquired by collectors and museums all over the world.

CHAPTER 16

Tea in St. John's Wood

IN APRIL DARIA MADE AN ABORTIVE ATTEMPT TO arrange a lunch for me to meet her parents.

> *April 13, 1939*
> Please don't come to lunch, it will be embarrassing, as I hate my uncle and he at any rate pretends to have a partiality for me. I have of course to be polite towards him and the family would never divine my feelings, and I could not bear the strain if observed by an alien eye. My mother was in the room, so I dared not confess this to you on the telephone. Please arrive at three, if you are not offended, and we can walk over Hampstead Heath, and perhaps you will have tea here afterwards?
> Very rudely, Daria.

For some reason I no longer recall, I was unable to follow this up and did not meet her parents until later in the summer. I don't have a record of the precise date. I did not give any thought as to which uncle Daria referred until I wrote my book about Mark and his three brothers, Jan, Boris, and Clement. It is unlikely that it was Clement, the youngest, also a pianist. He was considered an *enfant terrible* at the time, and it is unlikely that he was often seen in St. John's Wood. Later in his career he turned his back on classical music and took up jazz—no doubt to the horror of the rest of the Hambourgs—and is lovingly remembered today by nostalgic Torontonians as the genial patron of the House of Hambourg on Yorkville, a jazz joint frequented by students and others during the 1960s.

Nor is it likely to have been the kindly cellist Boris, whom nobody could hate. Daria was on excellent terms with him and later wrote to his wife, Maria, about me. I met both and heard Boris play many times as the cellist in the Hart House String Quartet. He was the director of the Hambourg Conservatory of Music on Wellesley Street, now the site of a public library.

So the detestable uncle must have been the violinist Jan. He was an odd character, somewhat of a dandy. He loved going to the races and never achieved prominence. However, he gained the respect of his fellow violinists as one of the editors of Bach's solo partitas, paying particular attention to the bowing. He married Isabella McClung, the handsome daughter of a wealthy Calvinistic judge in Pittsburgh. She was the intimate friend of the American novelist Willa Cather, who was a lesbian. For some years they formed a ménage à trois. Jan appears in at least one of Cather's novels. It is entirely plausible that he was the uncle Daria "hated."

Her next attempt to have me meet her parents succeeded flawlessly.

Friday morning [undated]
Please telephone me if you can on Saturday at 1:15. My parents will then be out.

I have obtained permission to ask you to tea here on Wednesday…The opportunity has at last arisen for you to meet my father, which you expressed a most earnest wish to do. Under the circumstances we shall not be able to talk much, or at any rate to say anything of great import. The only occasion I can see for doing this is on Saturday afternoon if you could bear to go for a walk in the park. I rather suspect, firstly, that you could not bear to, secondly that you will not be able to, and thirdly that your dislike of secrecy could in any case prevent you from doing so.

Clearly, Daria was continuing to play the Romeo-and-Juliet game. I was quite willing to play along and saw no need to tell her to stop it. Rather foolishly, I saw no harm in it. Evidently, one aspect of her game was her reluctance to present me to her parents. She was afraid they might not like me. I did not realize that for her this was not a game but a serious matter. No doubt I should have understood this, but I was obviously too dense to see it. In Mark Hambourg's autobiography, *From Piano to Forte: A Thousand and One Notes*, published in 1931, he showed that the Hambourgs marry upwards. Evidently, Daria was afraid that they would regard me, a poor refugee, even if I was a Cambridge undergraduate, an unsuitable candidate for the role of son-in-law. Mark had married up, and so had his younger brothers, the violinist Jan and the cellist Boris, who had chosen a prominent member of a military family that had been presented to the Prince of Wales.

When the tea was served in the living room of their house in St. John's Wood, Daria was silent. I attributed this to her congenital shyness. Her mother poured the tea. The conversation was unmemorable. Mark did most of the talking. I was not at all nervous; nothing was at stake for me. The occasion was significant only because now I had the chance at last to meet the pianist in the recording of the Beethoven concerto I had played so often at Cranbrook. As I expected, he had a Russian accent, but it was not strong since he was ten when he arrived in England. He was certainly formidable: a high forehead, horn-rimmed glasses. It was not surprising that a film director later wanted him to take off his glasses and play Beethoven. Probably no dialogue was required. In any case, nothing came of it.

I also learned from Mark's autobiography that he met his wife in the summer of 1907 in Belgium when he was visiting Jan, who was attending master classes at the summer school of Eugène Ysaÿe, the celebrated violinist to whom César Franck had dedicated his violin sonata. Daria's mother, Dorothy—"La Dolly," also a violin student—was lodged in the house of the village shoemaker—just the right ambience for a musical romance.

Nothing was further from my mind, as La Dolly was pouring my tea, that she would ever become my mother-in-law.

In fact, this was the second and last time I saw Daria.

CHAPTER 17

September 3, 1939

PRIME MINISTER NEVILLE CHAMBERLAIN:

I am speaking to you from the cabinet room at 10 Downing Street. This morning the British Ambassador in Berlin handed the German Government a final note stating that, unless we heard from them by 11 o'clock that they were prepared at once to withdraw their troops from Poland, a state of war would exist between us. I have to tell you now that no such undertaking has been received, and that consequently this country is at war with Germany.

You can imagine what a bitter blow it is to me that all my long struggle to win peace has failed. Yet I cannot believe that there is anything more, or anything different, that I could have done, and that would have been more successful. Up to the very last it would have been quite possible to have arranged a peaceful and honourable settlement between Germany and Poland. But Hitler would not have it; he had evidently made up his mind to attack Poland whatever happened. And although he now says he put forward reasonable proposals which were rejected by the Poles, that is not a true statement. The proposals were never shown to the Poles, nor to us. And though they were announced in the German broadcast on Thursday night, Hitler did not wait to hear comments on them but ordered his troops to cross the Polish frontier the next morning.

His action shows convincingly that there is no chance of expecting that this man will ever give up his practice of using force to gain his will. He can only be stopped by force, and we and France are today in fulfillment of our obligations going to the aid of Poland who is so bravely resisting this wicked and unprovoked attack upon her people. We have a clear conscience, we have done all that any country could do to establish peace, but a situation in which no word given by Germany's ruler could be trusted, and no people or country could feel itself safe, had become intolerable. And now that we have resolved to finish it, I know that you will all play your parts with calmness and courage.

CHAPTER 18

Refugees in the Blackout

THE END OF THE YEAR APPROACHED. MARGO AND Paul had their American visas and were waiting for space on a ship to cross the Atlantic in a convoy. To celebrate New Year's Eve, they invited me to accompany them to a party held in a large flat in an apartment house in Hampstead, around the corner from 20 Maresfield Gardens, where Freud had died three months earlier. The flat belonged to Oscar Wallach, an uncle of a school friend of Paul's from Cologne. Mr. Wallach, who himself stayed in the background, was a banker who had managed to transfer his money to England in good time and could easily afford to supply his nephew and his fellow refugees with seemingly unlimited amounts of champagne. This is why, if the celebrants had been able to remember the event the next day, they would undoubtedly have described it as the best Sylvester, the best New Year's Eve, they had ever had.

Amnesia the morning after had always been considered the ultimate proof of a memorable celebration. Everyone understood that, although technically we were at war, the war had not yet begun.

It was bitterly cold and the streets were covered with snow. The bus from West Kensington to Hampstead took ten minutes longer than usual. The Nazis had not yet dropped any bombs on London since the start of the war nearly four months earlier. Still, the blackout regulations were strictly enforced, and London was pitch black. This may have been unnecessary. Those who knew any Germans had reason to doubt whether any of them were sober enough to fly on Sylvester.

In Oscar Wallach's crowded and smoke-filled dining room, there was dancing to the sound of an excellent jazz pianist from Berlin. Paul had to raise his voice when he introduced me to his friends, Oscar's nephew Werner Wallach and his wife, Traute, who in turn introduced me to the girl of the evening, Jennifer Hill, an enchanting brown-eyed brunette, so far unattached, possibly the only English-born guest in the room. I could hardly wait until midnight—an hour away—to kiss her.

Her glass was empty.

"You look thirsty, Jennifer," I said.

"I am, desperately."

"I will put an end to this, come what may."

I looked around to locate the source of the champagne.

"You must feel rather lonely here, among all of us..." I searched for the right word "...aliens."

"I rather like aliens."

She had a delicious smile.

A refugee with a bottle wandered by. I asked him to fill Jennifer's empty glass.

"You don't have much of an accent," she said to me. I knew this was not true, but I was delighted to hear it. "How come?"

I explained the circumstances of my life, adding that I hoped that perhaps during the rest of the evening, she could help me get rid of what was left of my German accent. I said I knew of others who had not been in England as long as I had—by now nearly five years—who had got rid of it altogether. No doubt, with a lot of loving help.

"I will do my best. But if I were you," she said, "I would not wish to sound like an Englishman. A little touch of an accent will be of enormous help to you with the ladies. Look what Charles Boyer has achieved."

"All right." I put my arm around her. "I will keep mine just for you. Let's listen. I love that song."

The pianist had just begun Cole Porter's "My Heart Belongs to Daddy." An acquaintance of Margo's sang it with a strong Stuttgart accent.

When the applause had died down, the dancing resumed. Soon Jennifer and I were dancing cheek to cheek.

After a champagne-stimulated countdown, it was suddenly midnight. To demonstrate an advanced state of acculturalization, the pianist played "The Lambeth Walk." Unlike all the other males—including Paul, who kissed every lady in the room—I stayed with Jennifer. It was truly remarkable what her tongue could do. The effect was earth shaking.

"Jennifer," I stammered, "my heart belongs to you. Not to Daddy."

"You're not so bad either," she said.

No girl had ever paid me a greater compliment.

Soon food was served. Despite rationing, it was sumptuous, especially the sardine savouries and the salami sandwiches made with margarine.

Our glasses were filled again.

A happy refugee from Breslau approached, a friend of Margo and Paul.

"Are you aliens?" he asked.

"Less so every minute," I replied, giving Jennifer a squeeze.

"I want to become alien," she said, swallowing another gulp of champagne. "How do I do that?"

"Hopeless." The man from Breslau shook his head sadly. "You can work on it as long as you like, young lady. You'll never make it. You happen to be at a terrible, terrible dis-advantage. You're British. Sorry. Can't help you."

And he wandered on.

Jennifer and I went back to the dining room to dance. This time it was "Roll Out the Barrel."

After that we sat down, next to a man wearing a tux-edo and a red tie.

"What category are you?" he asked.

"C, of course," I replied.

"I could see it in your face," the man observed.

"Category of what?" Jennifer asked. "Male beauty?"

I happened to be well-informed on the subject of cat-egories. I explained to her that at the beginning of the war the government established 120 tribunals across the country to determine whether individual "enemy aliens" should be interned and locked up in camps right away or they could be exempted and remain free. Soon after the beginning of the First World War, more than thirty thou-sand Germans (who had not returned to Germany) had been interned in an atmosphere of acute Germanophobia and spy hysteria. But this time there were about seventy thousand refugees from Hitler's Germany in the United Kingdom, in addition to a sizeable number of German non-refugees. And there was very little Germanophobia. In 1914 no refugees from the Kaiser's Germany had come to England. Also, this time the government wanted to avoid mass internment, which in the 1914–18 war had led to much unnecessary suffering and was very costly. So the government established tribunals to determine, in a calm and unemotional atmosphere, who was and who was not loyal to England. They were often headed by members of the gentry who had no legal training. On the whole, they did their job as conscientiously as they could with the means at their disposal, and they bent over backward to be fair. But they inevitably reflected the values of the society from which their members were drawn. This occasionally led to somewhat odd results, although as far as I know they committed few, if any, gross injustices. The responsibility for the injustices that did occur, resulting in immediate internment, usually rested with the security organization MI5, not with the tribunals.

There was, for example, the case of Eugen Spier, a friend of Winston Churchill's who was now in the Cabinet as First Lord of the Admiralty. In the last few years Spier had seen eye to eye with Churchill and disapproved strongly of Chamberlain's policies. Inexplicably, MI5 declared Spier a security risk and he was interned.

There was also Bernhard Weiss, the social-democratic Jewish president of the Berlin police during the Weimar Republic, who was the target of a particularly vicious propaganda campaign by Josef Goebbels. Weiss escaped and settled in England. At the outbreak of the war, he was immediately interned together with a Nazi whom he had arrested ten years earlier. When the mistake was discovered, Weiss was released and henceforth treated like most other male refugees—that is, interned in the spring of 1940 and later released.

The tribunals dealt with sixty-two thousand cases of Jews, half-Jews, and non-Jews who still had German or Austrian citizenship. Among them, 486 were considered security risks, put in Category A, and interned immediately. In the cases of 9,314 aliens, the tribunals could not make up their minds. They were placed in Category B. That meant, among other things, that they could not travel without police permission, had to stay away from airports, and were not allowed to carry cameras. The remaining fifty-three thousand refugees were able to demonstrate their loyalty to England and were placed in Category C and exempted from all restrictions.

I was among them.

"What happened," Jennifer asked, "when you appeared before your tribunal in Cambridge?"

"The chairman," I replied, "looked at the dossier the Home Office had given him. 'Ah,' he beamed when he saw that I had gone to Cranbrook School. 'How's little old Pop?'"

I explained to Jennifer who Pop was. I then went on to describe my dialogue with the chairman.

"I told him that Pop was fine, as far as I knew, but that I hadn't seen him in a little while. He said he knew about Pop from the son of a friend of his who went to Cranbrook. 'Did you make the First Eleven?' he asked. My heart sank. How could I tell him that I had never understood cricket?"

"Don't aliens play cricket?" Jennifer asked me in mock innocence.

"They certainly do not! Allow me to continue. Would that condemn me to Category B? So I told him that I was a great batsman but perhaps not quite great enough. 'Never mind,' the chairman said with a benevolent smile. 'Even players in the Second Eleven can be loyal to England,' and he put me in Category C."

Traute Wallach, the hostess, appeared.

"I see you two are getting on all right."

"Not at all." I pulled Jennifer closer to me. "This girl is far too bright for me."

"That's true," Jennifer said and kissed me on the cheek.

"Too bad," said Traute. "I've always prided myself on my match making. I hope I'm having more luck with my other couples."

"There's one thing I want to know," Jennifer said after Traute had gone. "Didn't you and your friends object to having to appear before a tribunal? After all, you were Hitler's original enemies!"

"True, of course, but it never occurred to any of us to object," I replied. "We are aliens in wartime. We are guests in a country that has been good to us. It is fighting Hitler."

"Not yet," said Jennifer.

A woman with a double chin had been listening.

"It will be," she said, "once it has lost a few battles. Then it will pull up its socks. My name is Hildegard. What's yours?"

We told her.

"I haven't had such a good Sylvester since the Boer War."

"The Boer War?" we cried.

"What's so extraordinary about that? My father came to this country in 1901 to sell German leather. I was eighteen and in love with my piano teacher. So you figure out how old I am." She paused for a second. "Oh no, come to think of it, I had an even better Sylvester in the internment camp on the Isle of Man in 1916. And I wasn't in love with anybody."

"How strange," I said. "We were just talking about internment during the first war."

"You were? Let me tell you." She addressed herself to Jennifer. "You British had gone completely crazy. You destroyed a perfectly loyal, well-integrated, peaceful and highly productive community that had evolved since the late nineteenth century. You saw a spy for the Kaiser under every bed. There was no sensible reason for interning more than a few dozen people. The few spies the Kaiser may have sent over Scotland Yard could have found in five minutes, at any time. And put in existing prisons, not in new camps. Anyhow, if the Kaiser wanted information, all he had to do was ask his English relatives. Oh, the stupidity of it all! The Battenbergs had to call themselves Mountbatten. And Prince Louis, the First Sea Lord of the Royal Navy and the Earl of Mountbatten's father, was hounded out of office. But the yellow press demanded all of us be rounded up and put away. So the government obliged. It was convenient to have scapegoats."

"This time people are being more sensible," Jennifer observed.

"Yes, so far," the old lady said. "But if mass internment happened once it can happen again. If the conditions are ripe."

"Even for refugees?" Jennifer asked.

"Of course! Nothing easier than maligning them in the press. I could write the editorials for them. They're camouflaged spies. They take the bread out of our mouths. And they seduce the women away from our men."

"Oh no!" exclaimed Jennifer and poked me in the ribs.

"And most of them are *Jews*!" The old lady's double chin shook with excitement. "It's bad enough to be German—but to be Jewish as well! Obviously they've got to be put away. *For their own protection!*"

I never saw Jennifer Hill again. When she kissed me good night she gave me her card, which I still have.

CHAPTER 19

My Future, If Any

MOMENTOUS DECISIONS WERE FACING ME. IN A LIT-
tle more than two months I was to leave Cambridge. What
was I going to do then?

For refugees in Category C, the Pioneer Corps—
non-combatant units primarily for foreigners—seemed
to be the only possible way to get into uniform. Before he
and Margo embarked to sail across the U-boat–infested
Atlantic, Paul told me I should consider following them
and Robert to the New World rather than joining a "bat-
talion for inferiors" in the Old. He said I was soft in the
head if I imagined for a single moment that the English
would ever accept me as an equal, even after I was natu-
ralized. I replied that I had no illusions on that score, but
I felt more and more English every day, whatever they
thought of me. And I added that for more than a century
our crowd in Germany had felt more and more German

whether the Germans accepted us or not. Of course, we thought they had. That may have been an illusion, mere wishful thinking. Too soon to say, I said, with my customary worldly wisdom. One-sided love affairs were, after all, a common human experience and perhaps better than no love affairs at all.

Hundreds of refugees did join the Pioneer Corps, were subsequently admitted to the regular British Army, and fought. Some even became officers. Most likely, once in regular uniform the question of acceptance did not arise.

But for me, how could I think about my future when I had my final exams to worry about?

Then an extraordinary thing happened that seemed to take all decision-making out of my hands—an event to which I referred in my letter to Mr. Cecil Harper. One day early in March 1940, students were invited to apply to the Cambridge University Joint Recruiting Board to be considered for a commission in His Majesty's Forces. I saw no reason why I should not accept this generous invitation—I had already declared my intention to join up the previous autumn—and promptly filled out a form in which I stated, under the heading of "Nationality," that I was "German, i.e., a 'Refugee from Nazi Oppression,' fully exempted from special restrictions applicable to enemy aliens." I assumed that I would never hear from them again and forgot all about it. But now, to my great surprise, I received a card asking me to appear before the board the following Friday, at eleven o'clock, at Old Schools, near the Senate House.

I could not help it, but a number of rather disturbing questions arose in my mind. Did I really *want* to become an officer in the English army? Did I *want* to learn how to kill and prepare myself to be killed? Did I hesitate because I was a coward?

There was no question that I would do all I could to fight the Nazis. But how? Could I not meet my unquestioned obligation in some other way? Why did I not feel this was a Great Adventure? If others did, they did not show it. Obviously I would join up if I had to. But did I really want to *volunteer*? Why did I not feel the slightest urge to prove myself as a soldier, an urge that, from all accounts, my father felt most strongly in 1914?

Then another thought struck me with unexpected force: was joining the army the price I had to pay to become an Englishman? If the English would never accept me anyway, as Paul said, what was the point?

Suppose the board was more intelligent than the Aliens' Tribunal last autumn. Suppose they asked me whether or not I was prepared to kill the boys I had gone to school with in Frankfurt, some of whom had surely been my friends? Many of them no doubt went along with the Nazis because they thought they had to, not out of any conviction. Could I really say in good conscience that this did not concern me at all?

The board proceedings began with a short, polite conversation. After that, they wanted to know only one thing.

"Do you have any preference in which infantry regiment you would like to serve?"

I did not.

The four men conferred for less than a minute.

Their decision was unanimous.

The candidate, they said, was eligible to be an officer in the infantry. I cannot deny that I was a little pleased.

It meant, after all, that the British accepted me. I made this observation in a letter to Daria, who took a dim view of what had happened.

March 1940

I was pleased in these curious and unpleasant times to hear from you at last. I thought you had dropped me, flipped me away from your life in the most casual manner, just as one flips a bread-pill across the table. It was extremely offensive, but I never am offended, so as I say I was pleased to renew your acquaintance.

I wish you had not joined up.

Nobody but myself would have the impertinence or hardheartedness to say this to you, but I have no patience with hypocrisy and if you wish to continue our friendship you may as well know at once that it will be a friendship with a cynic.

Here are my feelings upon the situation. That it is a good thing that I shall not live to grow old, as I cannot imagine anyone wanting to live more than a couple of years in this world. You see, it is purely egoistic, but then what have you ever heard from me except pure egoism?

I don't think any war for any purpose is justifiable, no matter against whom or why. I'm not opposed to killing people, far from it, but I am opposed to killing the wrong ones, and, believe me, the only parties who are almost certain to escape alive and whole from this war will be the British and German governments who are now, they both state, fighting against each other. Don't write back and give me a good reason for war. I shall know it's propaganda. If anybody ever gives a good reason, a fair sounding argument, an ethical judgement in favour of war, then one can be quite certain it's propaganda.

I foresee all sorts of curious incidents arising from ideological warfare. Obviously the Nazi warplanes will bombard Stepney and drop leaflets in Mayfair, while the Russians will bombard Mayfair and drop leaflets on Stepney. Now, if you are flying at six hundred miles per hour you can't aim at anything with great accuracy, so the chances are that Stepney will receive Mayfair's leaflets and Mayfair will receive Stepney's. The results should be very enlightening.

Peace at any price, say I, believing as I do with Lao-Tse, "honour and shame are the same as fear." And even if they weren't I don't think them worth the lives of several million innocent people. You cannot but agree with me that for every guilty head at least ten blameless ones must fall.

CHAPTER 20

Tea with the Master

A WEEK AFTER MY APPEARANCE AT THE RECRUITING Board, E.A. Benians, the master of St. John's College, invited a selection of professors and students, all members of the college, to tea at five. He did this from time to time. Now it was my turn to be included. The invitation gave me my first opportunity to appear in public as a (potential) future officer in the British Army.

I had seen the master at the High Table in the dining hall, and I knew he was an eminent historian of the British Empire. But I had never met him.

Nor had I ever been in the Master's Lodge, but I knew exactly where it was. In my first year I had lived in college, on the east side of the River Cam. On the west side are the famous Backs, the pleasantly undulating lawns on which it is exhilarating to walk, and lie, and enjoy the view of the amazing medieval buildings. The graceful Bridge of

Sighs joins the sixteenth- and seventeenth-century college to the nineteenth-century New Court, on the west side of the River Cam. (It was literally a Cam bridge.) The Master's Lodge was on the side of the old college, the east side, separated from my Chapel Court by the large Master's Garden bordering on the Cam.

It so happened that it was already getting dark at 4:45 that afternoon, although it was March. In the black-out, dark meant pitch-black. I was, of course, wearing my cap and gown—this was an academic occasion for which they were obligatory—and carrying the gas mask that had been issued to everybody. In short, I had to find the Master's Lodge across the Master's Garden in total darkness. This was difficult but not impossible. It was remarkable how easily university life had adapted to the blackout.

Had I not recently been declared competent to be a killer and to be killed, I would have had no trouble. Normally, I have a good sense of direction. But evidently this declaration had seriously upset my psychic balance. It seemed that I now needed to prove to myself that the recruiting board was wrong and that I was, after all, unfit to be a British officer.

I was wise enough to avoid crossing the Bridge of Sighs, which would have led me to the New Court and the Backs. Quite properly, I remained on the east side of the Cam.

But I strayed.

I suddenly found myself *in* the River Cam.

I did not drown. I can swim. I climbed ashore. I was in no danger of being seen. Drenched and dripping I managed to run—no, to grope—my way through the Chapel Court, through the Second and First Courts, and through the main gate to St. John's Street. It was so dark that even the eagle-eyed porter did not see me. Then northwards to my digs. I changed my clothes. Fortunately, the student who lived above me was home and I could borrow his cap and gown. I kept the wet gas mask, probably useless now. A German gas attack was the last thing I was worrying about.

Having survived so valiantly an unscheduled baptism, I was completely at ease and in excellent spirits when I offered the master's wife my apologies for being twenty minutes late. I was forgiven, asked to sit down and offered a cup of tea. Two chemistry students arrived even later.

At the usual sherry parties, one stood up and wandered from one conversation to another. But at a tea party, one sat down, and there was only one conversation. Of the dons present I knew only two, the classics professor Martin Charlesworth, with whom I had friendly relations since he was a prominent member of the St. John's Musical Society, and Dean E.E. Raven, who once sat at my table in the dining hall.

When I came in, at the tail end of a general discussion about the way the war was going, the subject was the successful British boarding of the *Altmark* in Norwegian territorial waters. The *Altmark* was a supply ship of the *Graf Spee* that had been sunk in the River Plate in December on its way back to Germany. Norway was neutral. In breach of international law, the First Lord of the Admiralty, Winston Churchill, had ordered the rescue of nearly three hundred British merchant sailors who had been on ships captured by the *Graf Spee*.

"As no one knows better than you do, master," a venerable don with an untidy crown of white hair said with a smile, "the British Empire would not have become great if the letter of the law had always been scrupulously observed."

"George, I will answer that mischievous observation only indirectly, if I may," the red-haired Master Benians replied. "Only last week I was reminded by one of our local papers that it was God's plan to use the British Empire as an instrument to bring about a better world."

We all laughed happily.

"Speaking of God," one of the two chemistry students reported, "my vicar got into trouble the other day for saying in his sermon at Evensong that God loves even Hitler."

"Oh, He does," Dean Raven responded. "I only assume it, of course, from all the evidence at hand. I won't pretend to have any first-hand knowledge."

Inevitably, the conversation moved from the excellent prospects of the Lady Margaret Boat Club to the perennial subject of the status of women at the university. Women were not members and were confined to their own two colleges. But we men generously permitted them to attend lectures. Someone mentioned the old English scholar Sir Arthur Quiller-Couch, who enjoyed taking a firm stand against women. He always arrived in the hall immaculately attired and began his lectures, which were very popular among women, by addressing the audience as "Gentlemen."

"I strongly sympathize with him," a debonair young don joked. "I couldn't find a seat at the University Library last Friday. It was full of women! Awful." Like most of his colleagues, not to mention most students, he found Sir Arthur's antiquated position absurd.

Then there were the obvious complaints about the evacuees from London—from Bedford College, Queen Mary College, the London School of Economics and so on—for whom college buildings had been requisitioned.

"Speaking of the library," Martin Charlesworth said, "I hardly dare to admit this in the dean's presence, but I had a moment of deeply un-Christian delight yesterday when I discovered that there was nothing whatsoever to eat or drink left at the library tea room, unbeknownst to the fifty or sixty hungry and thirsty London students queuing up."

"But Martin, how did you know they weren't our own students?" the master asked.

"Instinct, Master," Charlesworth replied. "Instinct. One can always tell."

CHAPTER 21

The End of All My Troubles

ALL QUESTIONS ABOUT MY FUTURE AS AN OFFICER IN the infantry, and any other foreseeable future, were unambiguously resolved on Sunday, May 12, 1940, when two policemen arrived at 2 Richmond Terrace and very courteously and respectfully arrested me. The internment of enemy aliens, at first in areas near the coast, including Cambridge, was widely publicized. Daria assumed I was among them. During the following weeks the police carried out twenty-seven thousand arrests throughout the country.

The Nazis had invaded Holland on May 10. On May 11, Churchill succeeded Chamberlain as prime minister. The fourth item on the agenda at his first Cabinet meeting at 12:30 p.m. on May 11 was "Invasion of Great Britain." The discussion of that item led to my internment the following day. The assumption was that France would soon fall. After that, the Nazis would try to cross the channel.

It was feared that among German and Austrian nationals in England—enemy aliens—there were fifth columnists, Nazi agents, who had infiltrated the country. This, we were told, had been the case in Norway when they invaded that country in April. The *Daily Mail* and a few other papers had campaigned for the internment of enemy aliens, but on a limited scale. There was no anti-German hysteria comparable to the mood in 1914.

One thing that Churchill did was to shift the dossier from the Home Office to the War Office. The Home Secretary, Sir John Anderson, had done everything he could to avoid mass internment à la 1914. He thought it would be profoundly unjust to round up uprooted, defenceless exiles indiscriminately, especially since they happened to be Hitler's first victims. But under the threat of invasion Churchill dropped this restraint, wanting to convey to the public on his first day in office that the era of dithering was over. No doubt underlying the decision there was an element of anti-Semitism, even though by no means all of those arrested were Jews. There was a sizeable proportion of religious, political, and conscientious refugees among us who were not Jewish—how much anti-Semitism was involved is a matter of speculation contingent on the degree of paranoia one prefers. There is no reason to believe that Churchill was less anti-Semitic than other members of his clubs, even though he was in favour of the Zionist cause.

And what about the seven thousand Italians who were interned in June, after Italy entered the war? "Collar the lot!" Churchill said, according to the Cabinet's minutes.

The War Office was presumed to be more anti-Semitic than the Home Office. However, there is a school of thought that suggests that, instead of thinking of anti-Semitism as a contributory cause, we should look at the antipathy of English "club-land" to aliens in general and link this to a debate that had been going on throughout the 1930s about "Englishness." None of this, however, explains why relatively few women were interned. Mata Hari notwithstanding, the English seem to have thought that women were unlikely to be spies.

The official explanation was that we were interned for our own protection. Three months later, when the mass internment came under fire in Parliament, Churchill explained that in May and June there was no time for making fine distinctions.

Many members of the public were indignant. When C.R. Scott, my headmaster of Cranbrook School, discovered that three of his boys, now over sixteen, were among those interned—he did not know about me—he got in touch with several MPs he knew to complain. Regrettably, it was of no use.

Most of us were prepared. We had already appeared before the tribunals and had been put into one of the three

categories, most of us into Category C, the category of genuine refugees who, as I mentioned earlier, were exempted
from all restrictions. The tribunals' work was now declared
obsolete. A new situation had arisen.

Looking back, I should have considered what happened
an outrage. I should not have been so resigned, merely
because internment had solved so many of my problems.
I had some sympathy with what the government had done
in a moment of extreme danger.

My mother had a friend, Professor Mayer, who had
taught chemistry at the University of Frankfurt. He had
been in a concentration camp, but was released when his
wife could present an English visa. Once in the United
Kingdom he did war work, highly secret. This did not
prevent the police from arresting him. The idea of incarceration once again, however polite, was intolerable to him.
He went to the bathroom, opened a glass vial of poison,
and killed himself. My mother arrived in time to help his
wife clean up the glass splinters from the bathroom floor.

The rabbi-philosopher Emil Fackenheim was arrested
in Aberdeen. He had also been in a concentration camp.
Younger than Professor Mayer, he thought it made all the
difference to be arrested politely, to be called sir. He did
not object at all and considered the arrest entirely natural and justifiable, with the Nazis preparing an assault on
France. The police assured him he would be back home

in a few days' time, but he expressed his doubts. He proceeded to pack enough books for a year's reading. When they protested, he told them, "You know your business. I know mine."

When they came for me, however, I was not home. They spoke to my landlady, Mrs. Ridley, who thought of only one thing: if I was a German spy she would probably not get her rent money at the end of the month. (She did.) When I arrived home, I, too, was politely arrested. I hastily scribbled a postcard to my mother in London. It was against regulations for me to post it, so the policemen kindly did it for me. I could only imagine her reaction. I did not hear from her again until many weeks later. Of course, I was concerned that they might also arrest her. They did not.

The policemen did not, however, allow me to send another postcard to Anne Shorto, the sister of a college friend, with whom I had spent a glorious night of love in a small hotel opposite the Ely Cathedral—a short bus ride from Cambridge—the weekend before, just in time. That encounter was, in fact, so beautifully timed, and so magnificent, that it would have become the subject of a first chapter of another book if only Anne had followed it up with a flow of extraordinary letters. However, I received only a telegram from her, a week after my arrest. It managed to pass the censor and reach me, miraculously, in view of the general chaos. It read: "Darling, I have forgotten nothing. A thousand kisses, Anne."

Nonetheless, that note enabled me to live on my memories for the next year and a half behind barbed wire.

CHAPTER 22

Internment: The English Phase

I SPENT THE TWO MONTHS BETWEEN MAY AND JUNE 1940 in three camps: Bury St. Edmunds (in Suffolk, near Cambridge), Huyton (an unfinished housing estate near Liverpool), and the Isle of Man (between England and Ireland). During these months English forces had to be withdrawn from Dunkirk, and France fell. Italy entered the war. The danger of invasion became more acute by the day.

No newspapers or radios were allowed in the camps. We only heard about these events by word of mouth, usually by way of rumours spread by the guards.

Under normal circumstances we would have been in a state of acute panic, especially after it was whispered that the Vichy French had, after their surrender on June 22, simply turned over the keys to their internment camps to the Gestapo. Another rumour suggested that Churchill was going to ship us to Germany in exchange for British prisoners of war.

We should have been paralyzed with fear. But we were not. For one thing, we were always hungry. When you are hungry you think of only one thing. I mentioned this to Daria and received this reply:

June 2, 1940
Thank you so much for the peach you sent me. It smells so ripe and sweet, and is so round and soft in my hands, with its downy skin and faint yellow colouring. I think it would be coarse to eat it. I hope you will get my peaches and also the crate of strawberries and three churns of clotted cream which I sent to you.

I wonder what she would have written in response to our other fixation: the absence of cigarettes. Or to descriptions of the sanitary facilities, which were, let us say, inadequate. Or to our hastily improvised sleeping arrangements.

Most of us were young and were having a new experience. It was an adventure. Although the majority of us came, like me, from the Central European urban middle class, we found ourselves locked up with people we would never have met outside—wrestlers, a strong man who could carry a grand piano on his back (so he said), and a *Muskel-zwerg* (muscle dwarf) who was a Jiu-Jitsu champion. His amazing physique had enabled him to survive all kinds of horrors in Dachau. We had a professional juggler in the camp and an escape artist, universally known as Kletter-maxe, who tried it once and was caught. And there was Baron von Ketschendorf, who wore stiff collars, silk shirts, spats, and polished shoes. He had bushy eyebrows, carried a walking stick, and never forgot to put on a monocle for the roll calls (twice a day). There were a few farmers, Talmudic scholars, bohemians, poets, architects, doctors, artists of many kinds, actors, academics of all stripes, a violin virtuoso, a psychoanalyst from Vienna, and a Jew-for-Christ. And there were Nazis who, for once, were in a minority, but who thought, not without reason, that they were winning the war. We were lumped in with them, which did not mean that we talked to them. Or they to us.

The sociologists among us were able to observe, as though under glass, the formation of a class structure that paralleled the class structure in the real world. Also, lectures on dozens of subjects were organized right away. There was no shortage of scholars.

Our commandants would have preferred to deal with straightforward German prisoners of war to whom the Geneva Conventions would apply. Instead, they were stuck with a bunch of undisciplined civilians, most of whom thought that their incarceration was the result of a colossal misunderstanding. There were roll calls in the mornings and evenings. Although the common language spoken in the camp was German, those of us who had been in England for some time, especially the Cambridge crowd, spoke English.

The Cambridge crowd consisted of about eighty students and faculty who were regarded by many as intolerable snobs. Some of us were indeed more English than the English, which did not go down too well. A few sought the company of Count Lingen, the pseudonym of Friedrich von Hohenzollern, the youngest son of the former crown prince and grandson of the Kaiser, who was living in exile in Holland. (He died June 4, 1941, a year after our internment.) The handsome prince was in his late twenties and surrounded by a little court. He kept himself aloof from the crowd, but when he did meet us he made a point of being pleasant, whoever we were. Unlike other members of his family, he was not a Nazi, but neither was he a refugee. At Cambridge he had studied history with G.M. Trevelyan, but, so we were told, without much enthusiasm or talent. The prince had been in the German army and participated in the *Wehrmacht* tank corps in the annexation of Austria in March 1938. The military authorities, of course, knew he was related to the royal family and treated him with respect. I was not among those who sought his favour.

My father and grandfather had been court jewellers, not I. But I cannot deny that, for some strange reason, I was pleased to be in the proximity of a man who looked like, behaved like—and actually was—a genuine prince. Never mind that his grandfather had been deposed, and—Heaven knows—deservedly so. If his grandson had paid the slightest attention to me I would have been flattered.

We could not imagine when we would ever get out. Our sojourn was open-ended. Were we there "for the duration"? Or until Churchill changed his mind? Much of the talk revolved around that. Many thought they had "connections" that might facilitate liberation.

Of my three English camps, only one was prepared for us—the last one, on the Isle of Man, which had housed internees during the First World War. I only spent three weeks there. The other two were improvised. In Huyton there was a hole in the barbed wire. Two inmates walked through it and did a little shopping. When they wanted to return they had forgotten where the hole was. So they went to the main gate. They carried no identification papers—those had been confiscated. So naturally they were refused admission. "But we live here!" they pleaded. Eventually the guards took pity on them and allowed them in.

The requisitioned boarding houses along the seaside promenade in Douglas, the capital of the Isle of Man, would have been perfect for us had they contained furniture. But we managed somehow. There, rumours reached us that the Germans had landed in England. Few believed them. There was always talk that we might be shipped off somewhere, perhaps Australia or Canada.

On June 29, one week after France's surrender, I had written to my mother, who was in touch with other mothers and with the Refugee Committee at Bloomsbury House. "This may be my last letter from Europe," I wrote. "The rumour about Canada seems to be materializing. All we know is that those of us who are between twenty and thirty shall leave the Isle of Man for an unknown destination." The next few words were blacked out by the censor. "This letter is written on the assumption that we shall leave soon…We will have to do work 'that appeals to us' (the officer said so). What that means we don't know. I am prepared to do anything, go anywhere. The chance to get to the States seems considerable…"

Two days after I wrote that letter we were sent back to Liverpool and taken to a large hall. Lists of those selected to go overseas—unmarried men under thirty—were put up. The selection process was chaotic. Those who wanted to go could easily switch names with those who did not. I never heard of anybody who actually did this, but one has to admit it was a fine idea in theory. A number of men, far older than thirty, chose to go. Nobody objected. Fathers who wanted to go with their sons were allowed to do so.

Henry Kreisel, from Vienna, was sixteen. All he wanted to do in life was write poetry. His father objected vehemently. He wanted his son to learn a respectable trade. Naturally, Henry tried his utmost to get his father off his back so he could write in peace. When it was announced that young people could go overseas he was overjoyed. At last he could write! He was not amused therefore when, after both had recovered from dysentery, he spotted his father on deck of the S.S. *Ettrick*, which was carrying both of them, plus me, to an unknown future. Later, they were reconciled.

The *Ettrick* was an eleven-thousand-ton troopship, built two years earlier. It had just evacuated a number of people from St. Jean de Luz, including King Zog of Albania, and was now to carry 1,308 Category B and C internees, 785 German prisoners of war, and 405 Italians, far beyond its normal capacity, to a destination one hoped the captain knew. The passengers guessed it was Canada. The prisoners of war were given by far the best accommodation. The officers had cabins on the top deck. Few of us talked to the prisoners, but I heard that one of us met a schoolmate in their ranks.

We slept below deck in hammocks like sardines, without ventilation. During the first few days we were not allowed on deck. If a torpedo had struck, our chances would have been nil. We should have panicked, but we did not. I associated with an absorbing new friend, Helmut Könisberger, whom I never saw again but who, many months later, visited my mother on his return to England after his release. He became an eminent historian.

On the second day out we heard whispered rumours that a torpedo had struck our sister ship, the S.S. *Arandora Star*, which had sailed a few hours before us. The rumour was accompanied by urgent advice not to talk about it to anybody, to prevent panic. But panic was the last thing on our minds when, on the same day, dysentery broke out and long, interminable lines formed outside the toilets. It had become impossible for most of us to contain the eruptions from both ends. On the way to the toilets, one had to wade through oceans of liquid excrement and vomit. The stench was suffocating.

For some reason our prince and his courtiers had been spared and they were (unlike me) in the best of health, as was Hans Kahle, one of our older men, an impressive-looking, pipe-smoking, straightforward professional soldier who was a graduate of the *Kadettenanstalt*. He had joined the German Army during the First World War at the age of eighteen and then, after the war, became a communist. He became commander of the Eleventh International Brigade in the Spanish Civil War and a character in Hemingway's *For Whom the Bell Tolls*. Our prince, his courtiers, and Kahle got hold of rubber boots, brooms, buckets, brushes, and formed what was to become the legendary Latrine

Brigade. They got hold of enough Lysol to clean things up and procured paregoric to cure us. Within a day or two they earned the eternal gratitude of all of us who were stricken—and a place in history.

CHAPTER 23

Internment: A Camp with a View

MY MOTHER IN LONDON HAD REASON TO BELIEVE that I was among those who did not survive the sinking of the *Arandora Star*. On board the 15,000-ton luxury liner had been 712 Italians, 478 Germans including Nazis and Jewish refugees, as well as 374 British soldiers and seamen. Half of them drowned.

After two days, the refugee committee at Bloomsbury House gave her the news that I was not on the list of those who lost their lives. Daria found her address and was among those who expressed their happiness to her.

We were weakened and thirsty but exhilarated as we entered the Gulf of St. Lawrence, in glorious weather, on the tenth day out of Liverpool. It could no longer be concealed from us that this was Canada. Soon villages with church steeples came into sight and even human beings, Canadians. We were full of hope. What kind of work did they have in mind when they promised us that we could do something useful at last? One boy from Berlin sang *Wir fahren jetzt nach Kanada—da war noch kaana da* (We are now approaching Canada, nobody has ever been there), an atrocious pun (*kaana da* is slang for *keiner da*), and, as we sailed along the shoreline, one of our students, Werner Mosse, a cousin of my friend George, gave us a lecture on Canadian history. Nobody listened.

We did not know that, when Canada offered help and the British government accepted, the British told them they were sending German and Italian prisoners of war, and not civilian—mostly Jewish—internees. They suspected the Canadians might well have withdrawn their offer had they been told the truth. Few of us would have been admitted under the existing immigration laws.

That is why we did not receive a civilian welcome, and certainly not a civil one. In fact, one of the Canadian officers allegedly called us "the scum of the earth."

Naval vessels appeared from nowhere and accompanied us as we approached the Rock of Quebec, a stunning sight. Once we landed in Wolfe's Cove, the entire Canadian Army and Navy seemed to be there to welcome us, strongly supported by the entire Royal Canadian Mounted Police. After waiting on deck for some hours in the burning sun, during which a few of us fainted, we disembarked. Prisoners of war were separated from us, and so were the Italians, whom we had never seen on board. Buses, heavily guarded and accompanied by motorcycle escorts, drove us up the Rock of Quebec to the Plains of Abraham, in the centre of the city. As we stepped off the buses, a crowd assembled, amazed that some of the Nazi parachutists, or whatever they had been told we were, had disguised themselves as high-school boys, bespectacled professors, bearded rabbis, and rabbinical students with traditional earlocks. One captain heard some of us speak English and was heard to say to a colleague, "Yes, yes, I know. Those are the most dangerous ones."

We were taken to a barracks while our luggage was being "dealt with." Anything we still had on us, watches, cigarette cases, or pen knives, was impounded and entered on official sheets. None of it was ever returned. A few months later, the army conducted a series of courts martial, but none of us got anything back. From me they stole a rusty nail file, a comb from Woolworth's, and a pack of cards. When one of us complained that he had been deprived of a bottle of aspirins, he was told, "Never mind. In Canada you won't get a headache." When all this was over, we moved to Camp L, on the Plains of Abraham, with a gorgeous view of the St. Lawrence, near the Citadel, the summer residence of Canada's governor general, the Earl of Athlone, the younger brother of Queen Mary, and his wife, Princess Alice, a granddaughter of Queen Victoria, who happened to be our prince's godmother.

The commandant was Major L.C.W. Wiggs, a pleasant, well-meaning coal merchant from Quebec, soon to be nicknamed "Piggy Wiggy." A few hours before our boat arrived, he was flabbergasted to receive a call from Princess Alice, around the corner in the Citadel, requesting him, please, to be so kind as to tell the dear grandson of her first cousin, who was to be his guest, that she had called.

The day after we had settled in, Piggy Wiggy appointed our prince the camp spokesman.

After two months of under-nourishment in the English camps, the Canadian army rations prepared by our own expert cooks were excellent. And the army barracks—huts we called them—in which we lived were perfectly adequate. We actually slept in beds, not in hammocks, as on the *Ettrick*.

Clearly, we had no right to complain.

But complain we did—endlessly. Our complaints were all variations on one theme, the inability of the Canadian military to grasp who we were. It did not matter how often we stated the obvious: it would not sink in. Their misapprehension was dramatically demonstrated at the very beginning by our reception in Quebec. Piggy Wiggy had a heart of gold, and no doubt believed what our prince told him. (It was highly entertaining to watch the theatre provided by him and the prince: neither knew who should salute whom.) But Piggy Wiggy was not the problem. His superiors in Ottawa were. No doubt they thought they were doing their job conscientiously, looking after us to help the government of the mother country, which, at a time of great danger, wanted to unburden itself of enemy nationals on its soil. But it took them a long time to understand that we were not what they had been told we were, prisoners of war.

Once we were Piggy Wiggy's guests three interesting questions arose.

1. Should we agree to wear the POW uniform they provided—a blue denim jacket with a large red patch on the back and blue pants with a red stripe down each side? We refused. After long debates, we changed our minds and gave in.

2. Regulations provided that we were to write our weekly one-page letters or postcards on POW paper. We refused. After long debates, we changed our minds and gave in.

3. Should we accept the good offices of the International Red Cross or the Swiss consul who reported to the German government? We refused. This time we did not give in.

Before deporting us, the British had promised us—verbally—that we would be allowed to do useful work at our unspecified destination. But by now they had other things on their mind than request the Canadians to implement their rash promise. So we consoled ourselves by finding work, or at least activity, in two ways: by establishing a "Popular University" and attending it, and by conducting scrupulously democratic debates at our interminable hut meetings. Of course, in our spare time we were free to play with the soccer ball that our prince's godmother, Princess Alice, had sent to our camp.

Only about 60 per cent of the inhabitants of Camp L were Jews. The others were Nazis (presumably in Category B) whose primary home was Hut 14, and non-Jewish political refugees. The Nazis believed in the *Führerprinzip*, not in democracy.

This mix was just right for many exquisite exercises in applied political theory.

Should there be proportional representation in the senior meetings, with Nazis represented in accordance to their numbers, as "innocent" Piggy Wiggy required?

Should the Nazis be allowed to participate in the activities of the Popular University if they promised not to talk about politics?

Was Hut 14 to be allotted the same number of tickets as all the other huts for cabaret performances in the dining hall?

Should we give a hearing to a Nazi who wanted to follow Adolf Hitler's example when he wrote *Mein Kampf*—in his opinion the greatest book of the century—without any access to a library when he was incarcerated?

All this could not go on for ever. By mid-September the temperature was getting cool. Regulations did not allow the Canadian military to let its guests freeze to death. Only the dining hall could be properly heated. We had been told we would be split up and moved to other camps, perhaps merged with others, before the snow fell. Lists were being drawn up. We were ordered to put down our religion. Could it be true what we heard, that Protestants would be separated from Catholics? There were persistent rumours to that effect. Not just Jews from Gentiles. With that distinction, using a somewhat different vocabulary, we were only too familiar. One hoped the people here had never heard of the Nuremberg Laws. Separation between two different branches of Christendom? Why? And what about half-Jews? Half-Christians? What about quarter-Jews? Quarter-Christians? Agnostics? Atheists? If there were two or three destinations, and if space was a problem, were there no easier criteria? Why not just use the alphabet? Or the colour of hair? Or create a special camp for soccer players?

Max Perutz was a great science teacher at our camp school. He showed his students how to unravel the arrangement of atoms in crystals. He was willing to do anything not to be separated from his friend—let us call him Fritz—who was nominally a Protestant. Before the war, they had climbed mountains and gone skiing together, and shared girlfriends. Max wanted to stay with the Protestants because apparently they were to be joined to the Jews. There were many scientists among the Jews. Max wanted to be with them, never mind whether they were Jews or not. He came from a secular Jewish family and had been baptized Catholic when he was six. So after a surprisingly short search, Max and Fritz found Albert (another fictitious name), a nominal Protestant who for his own reasons wanted to be with the nominal Catholics. Assuming that rumours predicting something unpleasant usually turned out to be true, Max and Albert decided to swap identities. Max said, "We're just like the two swains Ferrando and Guglielmo in *Così fan tutte*. Nobody can tell the difference. So what if we are unmasked?" he asked. "Will we be expelled?"

Heaven only knows how the authorities eventually made their distinctions. In any case, Max would have been separated from Fritz if he had not pretended to be Albert.

In late September 1940 the time came to say farewell to Camp L. It was not easy because it meant saying farewell to the conducted tours (conducted by heavily armed tour guides) along the Grande Allée when we walked four in a row, like convent girls. Piggy Wiggy was proud of his city and wanted to show it off.

But the time came to move on.

CHAPTER 24

Internment: A Year in One Spot

THE LANDSCAPE—DRAB, UTTERLY UNINTERESTING. It was raining. We had already had some snow in Quebec, but it had not stayed on the ground.

After three hours, the train suddenly stopped. The guards told us we had arrived. We descended. This was not a railway station, we observed. But what was it? There were two sheds of some sort. And pits running through the sheds, filled with black water, along railway tracks. Soot was everywhere. The windows were broken. The roof was leaking. There was no sign of any beds. In the so-called kitchen, army rations were waiting to be prepared by our expert cooks. We discovered a few low-pressure water taps. No shower facilities. Six lavatories and two urinals, for use by 736 Jews and an unknown number of Protestants. No doubt the Catholics, we said, had more than enough gold-plated showers, lavatories, and urinals in their "Heaven" to accommodate the world's entire Catholic population!

Could the rumour be true that the real reason we were evicted from our Garden of Eden on the Plains of Abraham was to make room for Nazi prisoners?

We decided, at a noisy gathering in the yard outside the sheds, that we had no choice but to go on a hunger strike until we received assurances that we would forthwith be sent to a habitable camp.

My own behaviour was admittedly far from admirable. I watched and listened from a distance, standing apart from the excited crowd, feeling—what? superior? cowardly? too stupid to come up with a better solution?

Our prince did not want to be camp leader any more. Perhaps he was bored. The new leader, soon confirmed by the commandant, was Hans Kahle, the defender of Madrid.

He formed a committee consisting of Bruno Weinberg, an experienced international lawyer who had spent many years in Geneva with the League of Nations; two or three of our many doctors; one eminent architect; and our camp rabbi, Emil Fackenheim. (We actually had two rabbis, but Emil was the more eloquent.)

The next morning, on empty stomachs, they met with the commandant, Major S.N. Griffin. Poor man! None of this was his fault.

I was not present at the meeting. But I soon found out more or less what happened.

Kahle introduced his committee.

Weinberg rattled off the clauses in the Geneva Conventions and other laws the Canadian government had flagrantly infringed by dumping us here. He also told Major Griffin that British Ministry of Health prison regulations required a minimum of thirty-five square feet for each prisoner. He had quickly calculated we only had twenty-nine.

The doctors pointed to the stagnant water in the ditches and announced we were all going to perish in the very near future as a result of deadly diseases spread by the insects breeding there at this very moment. The architect said this place was unfit for human habitation and simply could not be fixed up. And Rabbi Fackenheim declared that if we were left here, all believers, Jews and Christians alike, were doomed to lose their faith in no time at all.

Major Griffin assured the delegation that he was doing all he could to improve matters, but that at this moment he was unable to give us the assurance we were asking for. He told them that his assistant adjutant, Second Lieutenant J.A. Edmison, had asked for permission to speak to the internees and, after listening to what he intended to say, he, Major Griffin, had given permission, on condition that it was understood by one and all that the lieutenant did not speak for him but only for himself.

So, in due course, Second Lieutenant Edmison climbed onto a table top to address us. He was the first Canadian officer we met who seemed to understand our situation. But just because of that, he threw some of us (including me) totally off balance, not merely because we were hungry.

He seemed to be a nice man, well-educated, smooth, a Montreal lawyer and alderman, in his late thirties. No doubt he meant well. He said he was acquainted with the Jewish community in Montreal. He was an honorary member of B'nai Brith and active in the Society for Christians and Jews. Before the war, he said, he had taken a strong anti-appeasement position. He said he had taken the trouble to find out exactly who we were. He knew there were many people among us who had been in concentration camps. He had every sympathy for our complaints. He considered them completely legitimate. But he assured us they would be taken seriously only if we cooperated. If we continued with our passive resistance, we would inevitably be the losers. Above all, we should not expect any help from the Jewish community in Canada, which was concentrating on trying to persuade the government to admit refugees from Europe who were much worse off than we were. This was an uphill battle. There was much opposition to it. The one thing the Jewish community would most definitely not support would be Jews who were, after all, safe, rocking the boat. "So—please cooperate!"

I found this an appalling argument, and so did many of my friends. We all accepted as sincere the officer's declaration of sympathy with our position. But he spoke as a lawyer, pleading the case for the military, a political lawyer at that, using any argument he could think of to break our will. We were not living in Canada; we were being held there. Nobody had ever suggested there was the slightest possibility of any of us ever being released in Canada. To tell us that by fighting for our rights, which he admitted were being denied to us, we were undermining the case the Canadian Jewish community was making for helping our fellow Jews in Europe was profoundly unfair, a hit below the belt. He was connecting two situations that were unconnected. True, some of us, no doubt, had written letters to Jewish organizations in Canada during the summer, complaining about our plight, but we all understood that the British interned us and only the British could get us out. We were, as it were, in British territory. The Canadians were merely caretakers for the British, and at the moment were not doing a very good job of it. Piggy Wiggy had done a good job. But that already seemed long, long ago. In short, we had no relation to the Canadian Jewish community. This officer was speaking to us as though we did.

We held a meeting. Those who thought along these lines were in a minority. The majority decided we should give up our passive resistance immediately and give them three days—until midnight October 19—to make arrangements to move us to a habitable camp.

Then we adjourned for lunch.

On the morning of the day before our deadline, Commandant Griffin spoke to us in the yard. To indicate to us how seriously he took the matter, he had written out his speech beforehand. He was the first to admit, he announced, that there was much to be done to improve conditions in the camp. If we worked together, we could perform wonders. Then he made his declaration. Sherbrooke was not going to be a temporary camp. "You and I are going to be here for a long time!" And then he made his direct appeal to us. We would get twenty cents a day for everything done to improve the camp. The only unpaid work would be for routine activities such as cleaning the place or doing the dishes.

"There are among you many clever and qualified men," he declared. "To them I throw out the challenge to assist in the planning and erection of this new camp. You will tell me what materials you need and I will supply them without delay...The winter is fast approaching and every day's delay is serious...Please stop talking and arguing. I speak to you not only as commandant but as man to man. I hope a lot of things will be different from now on."

When he finished he handed his written speech to Kahle.

Good, but not quite good enough, the camp decided. In any case, at the very least, we would have to be moved elsewhere while the camp was being made habitable. Newcomers from Camp Q wrote a formal letter to the commandant saying that he did not seem to be sufficiently aware of the gravity of the situation.

Whatever good Major Griffin had done was seriously endangered by another officer who suddenly appeared on the scene, Major D.J. O'Donahoe, a tall, red-faced Colonel Blimp. He also addressed us in the yard outside one of the two sheds. Immediately after his speech I went to a corner and wrote down exactly what he said.

Do you all understand English? (Yes.) You are here in custody. If you are asking for trouble you can have it, and plenty of it. I have very bad reports about you. Do not try any more monkey business. You will have to carry out every order you get. We have ways and means to make you do it. This fellow needs a haircut. (Hear Hear!) You are all Jews here. (Yes. No.) Well, that's all right. But you've got to wash; otherwise you get lice. We did not put you here. You just happen to be here. If you play ball, I will play ball. If you don't play ball, I won't play ball. That's all there is to it. I am not threatening you. I am simply stating facts. We are here to teach you fellows discipline. We have got nothing to do with your internment. We are only your custodians. Can you hear me? (Yes. No.)

You want us to win the war? (Yes, yes, yes.) We are going to start right here. Will you help? (Yes.) You are going to be asked—no, you are going to be ordered—to work, first woodwork, second sewing. Do you all understand that? (Yes. No.) Some of you have been in the business of making things. Well, we will teach you something useful so that when you get out of here by the end of the war, the time you have been interned will not have been entirely wasted.

This (he pointed to the shed) is going to be your home. (Laughter.) And you will have to keep it clean. Some of you may have a certain grade of reasonable intelligence. So you won't misunderstand kindness for weakness. We'll get you machines. Are there any people here who know how to make furniture? Joiners? Woodcutters? Tailors? I want to have a word with them.

This performance at first caused considerable confusion. Those who wanted to resume our hunger strike after the deadline expired insisted they were prepared to resist to the last man a combined assault of tanks and heavily armed Canadian troops storming the compound with fixed bayonets, with every intention to mow us down. However, they easily gave way to the Voice of Reason. In other words, we caved in.

The commandant turned out to be as good as his word. Within three days, armies of plumbers, carpenters, and electricians arrived, with carloads of building materials, blowing the wind out of our sails. Of course, the army knew far better than we did what was required. The speed with which they, with our help, for twenty cents a day, drained and covered the pits, installed new windows, fixed the roof, and constructed a coke-fired hot-water system with showers, toilets, and wash basins left us breathless. If we had moved elsewhere while this was going on we would have been deprived of an amazing experience. How fast they build things in the New World! No doubt skyscrapers did not take much longer. In no time, the kitchen was ready to accommodate the many chefs and pastry cooks among us, each claiming to have worked for the Ritz and the Savoy, not to mention the Café Sacher in Vienna. Major Balls, too, delivered. Machines soon arrived to equip several workshops. (We called him Major Balls since he had invited us to "play ball" with him.) Soon many of us were hammering munitions boxes, sewing kitbags, and knitting nets. I met the challenge by holding a rope, standing firmly on the ground while others risked their necks standing on ladders high up in the dining hall, putting finishing touches to the new ceiling.

But—horrors! A few days after the showers were installed, our two swains, Ferrando and Guglielmo in *Così fan tutte,* were unmasked. I never found out how. Max Perutz was summoned to appear before the commandant. Major Griffin, he reported to us, was impressed by the purity of his motives but nevertheless convicted Max to three days "downtown"—in the local prison. They locked him up in a cage resembling a monkey's in a zoo. No chair, no bed, only a wooden plank. However, he had hidden some books inside his baggy plus-fours—they did not want him to wear his POW uniform—so he was far less bored than the guard, who had to march up and down on the other side of the iron grill. His sleep was interrupted only by the occasional drunk. He was in excellent spirits on the day he came out. He later wrote about it in *The New Yorker* (August 12, 1985):

Unlike the prisoner in Oscar Wilde's *Ballad of Reading Gaol,* I did not look
>   With such a wistful eye
>   Upon that little tent of blue
>   Which prisoners call the sky
>   And at every drifting cloud that went
>   With sails of silver by,
> because I never saw the sky.

The sergeant major gave him a big welcome. He happened to like Max. I thought he also liked Klaus Fuchs, who taught physics in the camp school with Max. Klaus was silent, pale, and bespectacled—I think he was the son of a Quaker, and probably was a Quaker himself, a courageous opponent of Hitler. Klaus came from Rüsselsheim, near Frankfurt, was very left wing, and got on well with our pipe-smoking camp leader, Kahle, who was a proud communist. (Both men became famous later: Max Perutz shared the Nobel Prize for Chemistry in 1962, and Klaus Fuchs was the atomic spy.) Kahle was more jovial than the austere Klaus Fuchs. I was told that Fuchs was a superb physics teacher. He was not in my group and lived in a world far from mine. We never spoke, but we stood side by side several times during roll calls. For that matter, I had no personal relations with Kahle either, just as I had none with our prince, who was now very much in the background, protected from the mob by his courtiers, playing bridge most of the time. I heard he did not play very well.

Max and Klaus were lucky to be in the sergeant major's good books. His regime was totally arbitrary. He governed by bellowing. (He bellowed at me several times for not making my bed properly.) He was the tsar of all work programs, so naturally I kept out of his way. His name was Macintosh, and he was a big, red-faced bully with huge bags under his eyes and a tiny moustache right under his nose. He told his favourites that before the war he was a used-car dealer in Sherbrooke and hoped to be one again after the war. He was a Canadian patriot and boasted that he could not stand the British. (His origin was Scottish.) He could not understand why anybody would want to fight for them unless ordered to do so. He made no bones about disliking Jews. No anti-Semitism is harmless but, compared to the Nazi variety, his was noisy but touchingly innocent and without an ounce of malice. And, of course, totally ignorant. One day he asked one of our sixteen-year-olds whom he knew was not Jewish why he hung around "with all those dirty Jews." The boy replied that in a largely Jewish camp he had no choice. But, anyhow, the Jews were not dirty but very fine people. "After all," he added, "Einstein is a Jew." "Einstein? Einstein?" the sergeant major asked. "What group is he in?"

Our letters from England told us that the British public had been deeply shocked by the sinking of the *Arandora Star*. Up to that moment it had not been widely known that anti-Nazis had been deported and put at risk. Now there was universal condemnation. In mid-July there was a heated debate in Parliament. The government was put on the defensive. Soon it started releasing internees from the Isle of Man and from other camps. One week my mother wrote, confirming rumours I had already heard that the Home Office was sending a commissioner by the name of

Alexander Paterson to Canada to interview internees to decide whether they might be eligible for release in England under various categories, but primarily to ask whether or not they were willing to serve in the Pioneer Corps. I imagined my mother was very much afraid that I might go back and join the Pioneer Corps, for the obvious reason that I was safe in Canada and would not be safe in England.

But maybe I should go back to England? I mentioned this dilemma in a letter to Daria.

> *February 2, 1941*
> Whatever decision you make, I think you will be perfectly justified. Don't feel guilty. I do believe you are entitled to some sort of happiness at least. I know your mother expects you to go to America and certainly it would seem to be much the most sensible arrangement. If you will only let me know where you are going, I feel sure I could give you many introductions to people. My parents have so many American friends.

There was no chance to go to the United States, but a return to England was a real choice. Soon Paterson was due for a visit. I spent a terrible, agonizing week of indecision. I was constantly changing my mind, day and night.

I did not want to give any of my Cambridge friends a chance to lecture me on my obligations. I preferred to resolve this by myself. There was no argument in favour of going back that I could not think of myself—above all that I had a moral duty to do my bit and that I was not doing my bit by sitting in an internment camp being bellowed at by the sergeant major. Paul's argument that the Pioneer Corps was a unit for people whom the British did not trust was nonsense: it was obvious by now that one could graduate from it into the regular army. This raised the ancient question: did I really want to be a soldier? If I chose to stay, I had to accept that it was entirely possible, if not likely, that I would have to stay in this camp for the duration. The war was going abominably.

Then, at last, I made a decision, for the moment at least. I would stay. There was no prospect as yet of a release in Canada, but it did not seem to be entirely out of the question that the authorities could make an arrangement with the Americans.

Paterson arrived and spent two days interviewing candidates willing to return to England. Most of my Cambridge friends were among them. It was bitterly cold, but he did not wear an overcoat. Paterson was a nice man who had spent his life reforming the British prison system. He did not believe in wearing overcoats, he said. Two of us knew him from before the war. Walter Wallich, who, like me, had been a student at an English school like Cranbrook, had met him in Berlin during a school holiday through an English journalist he knew. Paterson was attending a prison congress at the time. He also knew another internee, the filmmaker Ernst Bornemann, whom he had met in London in connection with a film about prisons on which Bornemann was working, in which German prison experts were involved. Paterson recognized them both immediately. They had long talks. He confided to them that he did not think much of the military characters he had met in Ottawa. He did not bring with him any notes and made all the decisions—life-and-death decisions for those involved—primarily on the basis of his impressions.

Paterson worked fast. Those who were chosen were quickly notified. They were told they might leave for England at any moment. Several farewell "parties" (no alcohol, of course) were proceeding simultaneously, with speeches and lots of bravura jokes. I had to say goodbye to most of my Cambridge friends. It was painful. They assured me there would soon be another opportunity for me "to see the light." Paterson was to return to recruit a second batch. But I was not going to worry about that for the moment, especially since he had told several of my friends that he was planning to proceed to Washington, on behalf of the British government, to see whether those of us who had first-degree relatives in the United States could be admitted.

Among those leaving—our prince, Hans Kahle, Max Perutz, and Klaus Fuchs.

CHAPTER 25

Internment: The Camp Experience

August 12, 1941

I only want to tell you, though it sounds very Sunday School, that Kropotkin was at your age imprisoned for two years in a stone cell in the fortress of St. Peter and St. Paul, that he subsequently escaped, lived to have innumerable adventures (I don't necessarily mean the amorous French kind) and died some time after seventy in England.

I did not know when I received that letter—which certainly put me in my place—that Daria had a personal connection with the famous anarchist Prince Peter Kropotkin. I discovered this later. When Mark Hambourg and his family came to England from Russia—Mark was ten—they settled in Bloomsbury where many Russian exiles lived, among others Prince Peter Kropotkin, who became Mark's friend.

Our experience was somewhat different from the prince's, even though our camp song might easily have fitted the fortress of St. Peter and St. Paul. It was composed by Freddy Grant, who was already an accomplished musician when he was interned.

> You'll get used to it.
> You'll get used to it.
> The first year is the worst year—
> Then you get used to it.
> You may scream and you may shout
> They'll never let you out!
> It serves you right, you so-and-so—
> Why aren't you a naturalized Eskimo?

Whether or not we got used to it depended on our talents for living without women and being interned enemy aliens—or, after July 1941, friendly enemy aliens, i.e., refugees. The most talented were those who succeeded, one way or another, in conquering boredom. The young found this easier than the not-so-young. On top of the list of the young were the students of the camp school, who continued their interrupted education. Among the not-so-young were those who taught them. The camp school was an extraordinary success story. In due course, two or three enlightened military men and various committees persuaded the registrar of McGill University in Montreal to cooperate in this project. When the time came, our boys were transported to Montreal on heavily guarded trucks and allowed to take the matriculation exams. This would enable them to study at Canadian universities later, should they be released in Canada. It was an event of great significance, not least because after the exams the committees arranged a dance with scrupulously chaperoned co-eds, an occasion not forgotten for decades by any of the participants on both sides. As for me, I attended many superb lectures on a variety of subjects, outside the framework of the camp school, for which I was too old. But I did not know enough about any one discipline to teach in it.

Among the people with unusual internment talent was Helmut Kallmann, a tireless self-educator who made a systematic study of the speech patterns of the captured members of the German merchant marines who, for some strange reason, found themselves in our camp. For them that must have been an odd experience.

A fundamental distinction has to be made between two kinds of incarceration: our kind and prison sentences. Our kind was open-ended. Prison sentences have a predetermined conclusion. If we were behind barbed wire for the duration, we felt it was likely to be for a very long time. While we were in Sherbrooke, the Nazis were still winning the war. The battle of Stalingrad, the turning point, took place in August 1942, by which time most of us had been released.

However, there was at least one man in my crowd who thought the turning point occurred much earlier. The Nazis invaded Russia on June 22, 1941. When Heinz Kamnitzer heard about this, he announced to one and all that this was the end of Adolf Hitler. He would suffer the fate of Napoleon Bonaparte, he said. One and all thought that was pure, internment-induced wishful thinking.

As to my talent for internment, I could not compete with Kallmann, but until the last stage I managed reasonably well. I learned as much as I could from others and by reading. Somehow, there was never any shortage of rewarding books one could borrow—and discuss—and I enjoyed many new friendships. I relished the many superb concerts. Instruments had been provided by various committees. I tried hard not to be infected by the self-pity and self-centredness in which many indulged, and I was never angry with the British for what they had done to us, or with the Canadian military for being so dense about our situation for so long. I attributed this foolishness to all-too-human error. In my efforts to be worldly wise, I was perhaps too forgiving. There was probably more prejudice in British and Canadian attitudes than I was prepared to acknowledge. Arrogance helped me. I wanted to feel superior to the mob.

I had already had one very difficult period, trying to make up my mind whether to return to England and join the Pioneer Corps, as a number of my friends did, or to stay in the camp, waiting for American doors to open. For some weeks after the first batch had left for England, there was a possibility that this American option might actually happen. We had good reason to hope that, thanks to the efforts of Alexander Paterson, Washington might relent and admit us via Cuba. I had a valid American affidavit. My mother did what she could for me in London. But soon it became clear that the Americans would not let us in. Should I return with the second batch? After all, I had spent five years in England. I received a number of letters from Konrad Goldschmidt, a fellow law student at Cambridge, now in the Pioneer Corps. He made a direct appeal to me. He wrote I had a moral obligation to serve in the British Army. The Pioneer Corps was the way in. But, in the end, I decided again to stay and wait for America—not, I hoped, because I was a coward but because it seemed the reasonable thing to do, however tiresome the open-ended internment. Margo and Paul were by now in New York, both trying to find work, and Robert was still in New Orleans working for an import-export company.

As for my mother, the one good thing about her life, enduring the Blitz alone in London, was knowing that her three children were safe, even if one was interned. She did not know, as yet, that her mother was to be deported from Frankfurt and shipped by cattle train to Theresienstadt, where she was to die six weeks later. Until that news reached my mother, there had been hope that—through some miracle or other—Grandmother Kahn could find her way to New York.

My mother had recently suffered a trauma: her very good friend Kurt Stern had lost his life crossing the Atlantic on the way to join his wife in New York, when his ship was torpedoed. It was the second time his ship had been hit. The first time, a few weeks earlier, he was saved. At my mother's request, he was carrying a violin for me, which was lost—fortunately, not the good Italian one.

The possibility of my release did not arise until the middle of 1941, when attitudes softened and Canada at last recognized us as refugees. Suddenly internment was no longer open-ended, and the light of release in Canada began to shine at the end of the tunnel. But it was still very distant. That was the second time that life in the camp was very difficult for me. I found the waiting period intolerably long. All my high-minded aspirations of resisting self-centred self-pity collapsed, and I began to suffer from acute *internitis*, like so many others over whom I had tried to feel superior. I became impatient, irritable, depressed, and bored, experiencing a thoroughly unhealthy and unattractive combination of self-centredness and sexual longing, accompanied by a vivid sensation of having lost touch with reality.

It was the not-so-young who found the deprivation of life without women painful. Most of them were either married or were in "relationships." We, the unattached young, found it easier. Most of us had lively imaginations and consoled ourselves with imagined love. Besides, from the beginning we heard rumours that the authorities put sedatives in our coffee—"bromide"—that were supposed to suppress our sex drive. Some of us thought this was common practice in prisons. I have no idea whether or not it was indeed true. What is undoubtedly true is that one's sex drive takes many different forms and that there are useful and effective alternatives to heterosexual love.

Our sergeant major was the guardian of heterosexual morals and considered himself constitutionally authorized to suppress all alternatives. He had trained his men to go along the aisles, flashlight in hand, to make sure that there was only one internee under each blanket, both in the upper bunks and in the lower bunks. (We had double-decker beds.) My bedroom (Shed A) housed about eight hundred men, all of whom snored, but not in unison, so that there was a constant sawing noise. If the sergeant major's snoops found double occupancy, they chased the guest out. Someone said some time in the middle of 1941 that if in one year from now we were still here, the sergeant major would have to ask Ottawa for reinforcements because by then we would all have succumbed.

I fervently hoped I would not be able to participate in the experiment.

CHAPTER 26

Daria in No Man's Land

ON AUGUST 31, 1940, I CELEBRATED MY TWENTY-FIRST birthday in Camp L, on the Plains of Abraham in Quebec City. Now, in the summer of 1941, I approached my twenty-second birthday in Camp N, in Sherbrooke. By now we had refined a ritual for birthday celebrations: we had friends in the kitchen who supplied the raw materials, which helped. No alcohol, of course.

Throughout the year I occasionally received letters from Daria. The fact that I still have them shows how much they meant to me. They were a lifeline to the world I had left, a lifeline, I must add, to a world that was enduring the Blitz. Naturally I worried about Daria, as I worried about my mother. I was also concerned about Daria's incredible inability to keep a job—so incredible that it made me smile, the way one smiles about the trials and tribulations of a kid sister.

July 16, 1941

I know you must consider me a rotten friend. But I have had so little time in which to write lately as I am a nurse that I think perhaps you might excuse me.

The Wharry family has returned en masse from Switzerland, larger and taller than ever before, or perhaps it is only seeing them on flat land and not against a mountainous background. They arrived unscathed on the last boat to leave St. Malo. Shortly afterwards the harbour was blown up, in its way a rather fitting send-off, I think.

I am the worst nurse that ever emptied a bed pan. Forgive me if I am coarse, but, viewed unromantically, that is what my work chiefly consists of. I live in constant fear that I prove unequal to some necessary task. A few days ago I had to hold down the arms of a man who was being operated upon for an abdominal abscess.

O the trouble about me is that I would so much rather go to the scaffold than make my bed in the morning.

I might become a saint but I could never be a good bourgeois and I know that when my children scream I shall push them under a cushion and sit on them.

If I think to myself "what is activity," I can easily make all my energetic busy nervous little days, and all the forward energy of western civilisation seem meaningless. But what does one meditate upon except ceaseless activity, and if this were not, what stuff would there be for meditation?

Of course it is hard for you, an altogether unnatural life without any purpose to console you, for instance if you were suffering for some religious or political cause, and you have always been a sociable person. If only you could undertake some long study which would really absorb your whole interest. I can't suggest what, but there must be something. Surely that is a problem—how to be creative in one's life, without stimulation from external sources to which one has been used. I watch your struggle with as much hope and fear and anxiety as I do the struggle of my friends who are fighting in the war. I'm not sure that yours is not the more heroic task.

I have my problems, too, the personal kind, how important they are! But some of them are so trivial that you would laugh long and loud if I related them to you.

You must know that I'm making every effort to help you from here, but it's darned hard. Most influential people have ears of flint and hearts of wood, their heads are small.

Alas, or shall I say, rejoice, I have lost my job. And it began so propitiously with an encounter with Julian Huxley in the gentlemen's lavatory, surely the oddest place in which to meet a distinguished personage. Forgive me if I am coarse again, but it was rather ironical and I laughed about it a great deal at the time.

Tomorrow I am going for an interview to see whether or not I can become a social worker in London. You know, how I have always longed to do this.

Imagine me waddling down Whitechapel High Street in large flat shoes in a large flat hat to inspire confidence, drinking syrupy tea out of cracked mugs in sordid little rooms, nursing dribbly babies, pinching the cheeks of unhappy children and giving advice on any subject.

Three weeks later Daria wrote me this letter:

August 7, 1941
I have now changed jobs for the tenth or is it eighth time in one year, and am working, much to my astonishment, as a translator of the *Zeitung*

newspaper. My new boss is one Lothar, known to your mother in Frankfurt.

And five days later, this:

August 12, 1941
I have now lost my ninth job. There must be something extraordinary in store for me, as Clive of India remarked when he fired the third dud bullet at his temple and nothing happened.

CHAPTER 27

German Lessons

AFTER GIVING UP THE FLAT IN NORTH END HOUSE IN
early 1941, my mother lived in the Ormonde Residence in
Hampstead—throughout the Blitz. Margo and Paul had
left in a convoy to the United States. Uncle Ludwig moved
in with his sister, also in Hampstead.

My mother regularly wrote to me, often mentioning
that she went down to the shelter during a raid. She related
this in a matter-of-fact voice, without emotion, no doubt
partly because she did not want to worry me, but I think
the real reason was that she was so traumatized by the loss
of two husbands and by her emigration—having to leave
her mother behind—that nothing that was happening now
had much significance.

April 1941
I now have German lessons with your mother. We

get very excited. Because I perpetually embark upon
seas of Shakespearian eloquence, am carried away,
relapse into English and finally talk a mixture of pid-
gin German and Teutonic English, which she strives
to translate and rationalise. I can never keep politics
out of the conversation, though I detest them, and
continually make remarks to her about the deca-
dence and stupidity of the rich, and then suddenly
remember your family history and feel very embarrassed! I at last understand something which used
to bewilder me in the past, namely that you did not
hate home life or find it difficult to live peacefully
with your family. She is quite different to any person
of the last generation I have yet spoken with: she is
so unartificial and is interested in everything and
knows a great deal but never talks in a patronising
way. In short, she talks my language, as you did,
and also has a similar sense of humour to mine.

My mother, too, wrote to me about the lessons.

March 7, 1941
Daria came and had tea with me yesterday. She
wrote to you, so you know all her news. They seem
to be pretty badly off. She is very much looking for a

job but apparently with no success anywhere as yet. She asked me if I would give her German lessons. She would pay me as soon as she had a well-paid job. I said I would not give any lessons on credit, but in her case I would love to do it without payment, which she said she could not accept but then decided to after all. We shall begin on Monday. I wonder whether she will do it seriously. If she gets a job she will probably have to stop. She is unchanged: when she left she asked me for 2d for her fare home, being late. But she must have had some money before, as she brought me some snowdrops!

March 12, 1941
Daria rang me up. She wanted to come for her first German lesson, telling me that she had a job in the *Times* library. She very much wanted to take the lessons, but she was only free on Sundays. So she will come Sunday morning. I think it is a lovely job for her.

March 20, 1941
Daria really turned up Sunday morning for a lesson and intends to come regularly. She really is a nice

and clever girl. She does not pay, of course, as she only gets 13/6 a week in her job! She does not like it, of course. She helped me looking for your music in your trunk.*

April 11, 1941

Daria came for a lesson again this morning (Good Friday). I like her. She asked me if she could say *Du* to me. It was very sweet of her, but from the pedagogical point of view I should not advise it; speaking German she would most of the time have to say *Sie* to people. Of course she always forgets her book, or work, or something. She has sent some recommendation letters for you for some friends of theirs to Margo: she said she had written to you about it. She gets me books to read from her library, where I went to see her the other day, on very cheap terms, [for example] *Kitty Foyle*, which Robert recommended to me. She does speak German funnily. She says "*Ich muss meine Schwester aufklingen*," or speaks of

---

* My mother sent my music to the camp at my request. It duly arrived. It was used by others. I never played the violin behind barbed wire. I was in the company of too many good musicians and was embarrassed.

"*Mein Affe*" meaning "*Mein Neffe*" (whose name by the way is Mark Anthony).[†]

May 8, 1941

Daria comes on Sunday mornings. This time she was an hour and a half late, having not considered the new summer time. Evenings are not so long now. Today's blackout: 10:20.

May 22, 1941

Last Sunday Daria invited me to a Mahler concert in Wigmore Hall. No orchestra, mostly singing. It was lovely! Mostly Germans there, I guess. Mahler is not very much known here.

June 14, 1941

Daria was here again yesterday. She now comes in the evenings, so as to be free on Sundays in summer. For the first time in weeks she had not forgotten her book. She brought me some lovely lilacs from the garden.

[†] Mark Anthony, the son of Nadine and Tom Marshall, went on to serve in the British foreign service as ambassador to Yemen.

June 28, 1941

Last week Daria did not turn up for her lesson. This week I got a nice letter excusing herself for not having posted it in time (six days late). And then she had forgotten to put stamps on the letter. She has a new job, she says, which makes her too tired at present—but she hopes to come again after a while. She does not say what kind of job it is. I shall ring her up in a few days.

July 4, 1941

I spoke to Daria on the phone last night. She works in an office called "political and economical training" and seems quite happy there. She would like me to come for tea next weekend and wants to take up her lessons again in a week or two. I spoke to Michal, too, who lives with them now, with her husband.

August 8, 1941

Unfortunately, Daria has already lost her newspaper job again, after a week's trial. Her German was not good enough, which I feared too. And I am afraid she is too much of a *Schussel* [scatterbrain]. So for the time being she again can't pay for her lessons,

and won't come so often either, having first of all
to look for another job.

October 11, 1941
Tomorrow I am getting a new pupil for German, a
cousin of Daria's, a Miss Ogilvie from Scotland. I
am very pleased and wonder what she is like. Very
nice of Daria. She really is a good friend and seems
to think a lot of my lessons.

October 17, 1941
Miss Ogilvie came for her lesson already and she
wants to pay well, too. She does not know any German, but is nice and intelligent, your age. She has
only arrived here recently and is going in for nursing, so unfortunately she has only so much time.
She lives in a convent and seems to enjoy it. I really
think this is the occupation I am suited for best.

A letter from Daria to my mother:

March 16, 1942
Dear Mrs. Netter,
I fear that, as is all too frequent an occurrence, I
owe you a profound apology. The Sunday I intended

to come to you for a lesson I developed flu. I asked my landlady to phone you, but she forgot to do so. Subsequently I was sent on a motor-cycling training course which entailed leaving the house at 7:30 and returning at 8. I forgot myself to 'phone you and now I do not dare as I feel you must be most angry and offended with me, which unfortunately you only have too good reason to be. This past week I have been laid up with a blister (septic) but I hope to return to my bicycle by Thursday.

I shall ring you up over the weekend. Please forgive me. What seems to you my rudeness is a kind of blanket fog which sometimes muffles up my mind for a few days just after I have made a noted improvement in practical details and have prided myself on my ability to cope successfully with day to day existence without forgetting or neglecting any of its essentials.

I cannot think of any way to apologise to you, for whom I have such respect and who have helped me so much, except to say please forgive me.

Daria

CHAPTER 28

A Benevolent Colonel

ON JULY 12 I WROTE A DEPRESSED LETTER TO MARGO and Paul. We had just been told, after our hopes had been raised again and again, that immigration to the United States was, after all, impossible. I did not expect the improvement that came with our recently declared official status as refugees would amount to very much. I told myself—not entirely convincingly—that new rules about working would cut into my spare time, which I needed for my legal studies—by now I had, of course, abandoned any idea of being able one day to resurrect the Koch jewellery business.

Since the possibility of release in Canada appeared to be non-existent, I intended after all to go back to England with the next batch. I was not going to tell my mother: there was no need to worry her about my crossing the Atlantic. I was going to surprise her once I arrived. In England I hoped to be released in one of the civilian categories rather than having to "yield to a recruiting officer." That phrase enraged Paul nearly as much as the reason I gave for it, stupidly, that I was "really a civilian at heart."

Unfortunately, a censor happened to see that letter and pounced on it. He underlined a number of offending passages and sent the letter to his boss, Lieutenant Colonel R.S.W. Fordham, Commissioner of Refugee Camps, who sent it on to Margo and Paul. He pointed out to them (they sent me a copy of his letter) that the underlined statements were "either untrue, improper or unfair" and went on to say that it was

> sometimes very difficult to make certain refugees comfortable and happy in any sense of the word as instances occur where they seem anxious to find fault or complain, and it is feared that the present example was such a case. Actually, many changes have been made of late for the benefit of refugees, and it is probably correct to say that nowhere are they treated better than in Canada. When Mr. Koch writes a letter of this character he incurs the risk of having the question of his allegiance adversely viewed. Nevertheless, the letter is being forwarded to you rather than withheld, and the writer is being

> asked to be more careful in future about what he
> puts on paper.

Margo and Paul were greatly upset, but not as much as I
was. I realized, of course, that I had gone too far. And I
understood that my allegiance was being questioned and
that this was to be taken most seriously. The implications
were obviously horrific. The door to Canada would not be
opened. Who knows what they would do with me then. In a
letter raising hell with me, Paul suggested I write a letter to
Lieutenant Colonel Fordham setting things straight, point-
ing out to him, among other things, that the Cambridge
Recruiting Board had decided I was officer material and
that, of course, I was willing to serve in the British Army.

I followed his advice.

What ensued was truly remarkable.

Suddenly Pop—my house master at Cranbrook, the
dwarf with the giant intellect—once again became a character in my story. It so happened that he had a brother,
Jack, an eminent economist high up in the British High
Commission in Ottawa. Pop had written to his brother
about me, hoping that he and his wife, Honour, could do
something for me. So, a few days after the letter incident,
they met Lieutenant Colonel Fordham at a dinner party.
Jack Osborne told him that one of his brother's former
pupils, Otto Koch, was in his care. Fordham recognized

the name immediately. He probably also mentioned my letter. In any case, a week or two later, when he visited the camp, I was called out to meet him.

Of course, I feared the worst. However, there was no need. On the contrary. He turned out to be an affable, agreeable man, a lawyer himself, and a human being as well. He confirmed what had already been rumoured in the camp, namely that a possible release in Canada, under one category or another, may, after all, not be entirely impossible for us, some time in the indeterminate future. One category was for students, but they had to be under twenty-one, which left me out. There was certainly no category for lawyers. "Lawyers in wartime are an unnecessary evil," he said. "I am a King's Counsel myself, and I have dropped my practice for the duration. You should learn something useful." I said I hoped to take a course in draughtsmanship. I had always thought that learning to do something with one's hands was a good idea and I admired those who had mastered it. "Very good, very good," he said and the interview was over. I think he summoned me only out of curiosity. He did not mention the Osbornes. They wrote to me about meeting him only afterwards, when they confirmed what I already suspected—that, after our situation was cleared with the British government, our fate was now entirely in Fordham's hands. It was he who would have to decide, when the time came, whether I could be released in Canada, provided that a Canadian could be found to assume the necessary financial, legal, and moral responsibilities as sponsor.

The door to Canada was opening.

Until my interview with Lieutenant Colonel Fordham there had been no end in sight—up until that point, the only chance to be released (other than returning to England) seemed to be in the form of immigration to the United States, and Jewish organizations constructed all kinds of schemes to make this possible, via Newfoundland or Cuba. Margo spent a lot of time on this. It was frustrating because I was only a few miles north of the American border.

Suddenly there seemed to be two possibilities, one of which lay right outside the camp's bounds.

But the American option soon faded away. As to Canada, the waiting time between the opening of the door and my actually going through it became almost unendurably long. This last phase of the internment was unquestionably the hardest. By July 1941 I had been interned for fourteen months.

Today, more than seventy years since my internment, I find it is easier to remember the good things, the friendships, the intellectual stimulation, and, most important, the experience as such—a greatly enriching event in my life. Did it include suffering? Yes, it did—and in this last phase most definitely, so much so that it affected my judgement in a fundamental way. Had I not suffered, I would not have written the silly letter to which Fordham took exception. (One would have thought he might have had better things to do than waste his time on it.) I was very much aware of the effect that internment was having on me at that stage. The word for the self-pity, boredom, and irascibility from which I was suffering was internitis.

Although Daria called this condition "heroic," she was considerably off the mark.

CHAPTER 29

The Consequences of Internitis

I WAS NOT AWARE OF ONE PARTICULAR ASPECT OF internitis, however—a distorted view of my relationship to Daria. The longing for my release made me start to see her in a new light. In my imagination—and soon not only in my imagination but also in my letters—she had become, in a peculiar and somewhat blurred sense, a love object. My letters took a romantic tone in those weeks before my release and for considerable time afterwards. But her responses made it clear that the time had not come for anything resembling a permanent commitment. For one thing, she must have known that her parents would not have welcomed a rootless refugee whose family may have had a past but, from what anybody could tell, certainly had no future. But if one leaves that aside, the circumstances of Daria's life—the life of a marginally employable bohemian in wartime England, a proud member of a well-established family but who saw herself as a strong rebel against the bourgeoisie—were hardly conducive to long-term planning.

This was evident in her response:

September 6, 1941
You see, you make my task very difficult because I can't tell whether or not you were drunk, and, if so, it would be very unfair to take advantage of it. I mean, how I am to know that two or three days later you might not have thought "My God, what did I write to Daria? How shall I explain it?" And felt yourself compromised.

Your "indecent" suggestion—why "indecent"? With such barriers of land and sea between us, there is little possibility of it ever being put in effect. But I shouldn't consider it indecent. Perhaps I might even be glad.

I promise not to arrive at Camp N one morning armed with breach of promise suits and a large suitcase and a hatbox full of mementos and claim you as my husband. So be content and kindly trust me in future.

You say that you love me, but perhaps you will change your mind. Also there is so much against it, and so many things may happen. And for my part

I am certainly very fond of you and eagerly await news of you, and have much in common with you, but more than that I cannot say now.

I have such firm ideas about these things. I do believe when two people love one another that should include the world and the most important [thing] is not mutual egoism, though that is a part, but sharing of ideals and knowledge and love of other people.

"There probably is no God but at least I shall act all my life as if there were" is an irrational philosophy, but one has to wear the shoes which fit one's feet and can throw them away once they are outgrown.

My letters were not consistent. Sometimes I struck the wrong note.

September 11, 1941
I should be rather offended if you thought of me as a younger sister. It would wound my enormous vanity.

In the same letter she gave an extraordinary description of herself:

You know, you always speak to me and of me as if I were English and I never will be. I have a profound respect and love for the country in which I was born and brought up, but I never feel myself truly to be one of them or at one with them. It is extraordinary how strong is the influence of my heredity.

When news reached Daria of my approaching release she was genuinely happy for me.

October 20, 1941
Now, I think, I do think, you are to be released. It is not necessary to tell you how delighted, relieved, excessively, superabundantly, overwhelmingly glad I am of this. Go—my dear young sir—assume your peruke and put on your horn-rimmed spectacles and wag your legal finger at the world. But in your spare time, please don't have too many too serious love affairs with these fast young Canadian women, ostensibly because it will distract you from your work, but in reality because I am jealous. My nature is pleasant, amiable and kind, I do not bite, I expect people to slap my right cheek and quite often I offer them the left as well, but I am an ordinary "'uma-nbein" and my feelings are the same as any others.

The elephant shelter at the London Zoo has been converted into an air raid shelter.

In her letter of August 7, 1941, she wrote:

> I have been very busy and agitated this week and among other things have written to my aunt (Mrs. Boris Hambourg, 194 Wellesley Street, Toronto), telling her about you and asking her to give you all possible assistance.

CHAPTER 30

A Love Story

I WAS NOT THE ONLY ONE BEHIND BARBED WIRE WHO entertained romantic thoughts. There was also the case of Peter Field. The object of his desire was considerably closer than mine.

His story began the previous summer. There were two walkways along the barbed wire and watchtowers surrounding Camp L in Quebec City, Piggy Wiggy's camp, in which we spent the summer of 1940, one close to the compound and the other twenty metres, a shouting distance, away. Curious Quebeckers could stroll along the outer walkway and inspect those of us who happened to be visible, and if they shouted we could hear them, and vice versa. Of course this, or any other communication whatsoever between them and us, was strictly forbidden.

Nature was prodigiously generous to us. The view from the camp of the valley of the St. Lawrence below, and of the villages with their church steeples on the other shore in the distance, was glorious. It provided the perfect backdrop to the tender love story I am about to tell. Everything around us was sumptuous. The St. Lawrence was mightier than the Rhine and the Danube combined, not to mention the Volga, the colours brighter, the sunsets more intensely blood red, and the thunderstorms noisier than those at home. And, as has been mentioned before, the camp was located on the Plains of Abraham, the only world-class battlefield in Canada, where in 1759 the English beat the French, and the future of Canada was decided. This made us feel as important as if we had been incarcerated on the battlefields of Waterloo or Gettysburg.

One of the curious Quebeckers who walked along the walkway was Pauline Perrault, a blond school girl of fifteen who lived in her grandfather's house on the Grande Allée, the most fashionable street in Quebec. The grandfather was the Liberal senator Charles Alphonse Fournier, a friend of Prime Minister Mackenzie King's, noted for his resemblance to Sir Wilfrid Laurier. He doted on Pauline. Her parents were separated. Her mother and aunt also lived with her.

It so happened that the camp was on the route between the Grande Allée and Pauline's school. So, by making only a small detour, she could focus her attention on the man of her choice—Peter Field.

Pauline had good taste. Peter looked like a Wagnerian tenor—handsome, blond, imposing. He was *old*, twenty-six, and came from Vienna. He had been a book salesman in Germany, Poland, and Holland before the war. From Holland he made a hair's-breadth escape, only to be interned in a Liverpool barracks, in his words a real hell hole. But he did not mind. He was amazed he was still alive.

By September, after I had celebrated my twenty-first birthday in excellent company, a time when the leaves were just beginning to turn and the valley of the St. Lawrence was golden and several of our poets were polishing their sonnets in praise of the Canadian autumn, the relationship between Pauline and Peter had matured from an exchange of amorous blowing of kisses to an exchange of amorous notes—and more. All this began with the help of one of the guards who had been watching.

"You like Blondie?" he asked Peter one day. "She enquired about you."

Peter did not believe him at first. He thought he was teasing him. But then the guard wanted to know whether he would like her name and address. He said yes, of course. If he would get it for him Peter would give him his penknife.

This was considerable progress from the time when he had shouted hello to Pauline. But he suffered a temporary setback. A different guard had Peter arrested and thrown in the clink for a few hours.

A few days later, the first guard told Peter that he had the address. Afraid of being seen giving it to him, the guard dropped the piece of paper on the ground; Peter picked it up and dropped the penknife on the same spot.

Not long afterwards, we were moved to Camp N in Sherbrooke, three hours away by train. A regular correspondence ensued, in English. Pauline's English was better than his French. I did not know Peter well at the time, but we later became friends and he told me many things I did not know. It was easy for me to understand that Pauline developed a schoolgirl's crush on Peter. After all, what is more romantic than a handsome prisoner languishing behind barbed wire? It was just as easy to understand that Peter was immensely amused, and flattered, by her attention, especially since it was also a public entertainment.

But it was not quite as easy to understand that he would become serious. He told me, and no doubt everybody else, that he would write a letter to the commandant asking to be let out, just for a few hours, on his word of honour, and be allowed to visit the girl. He said he would go mad if the commandant said no.

He did not write that letter, and he did not go mad, or rather not madder than the rest of us whose mental health had been grievously undermined by not having seen a live woman, except on the distant, outer walkway in Quebec City, since May. But he did write to Pauline, now that he had her address, and she wrote to him, many times. The censors must have enjoyed reading the torrid letters. She sent him photographs of herself, posing on the monuments of generals Wolfe and Montcalm, the fallen heroes of the Battle of Quebec.

Many months later, more than a year after Pauline had first blown a kiss to him, it finally became possible for friends, relatives, and others to make arrangements to visit us. By this time, we were in Camp N in Sherbrooke, which had been designated a refugee camp.

In due course, Pauline, her mother, and her aunt came from Quebec City to visit Peter.

"About eight hundred guys," Peter refreshed my memory of the scene later, "pressed their noses against the barbed wire to watch the scene. She did all the right things. She ran towards me, fell into my arms, and kissed me. She loved every minute of it and played it up to the hilt. The men just howled. We must have been together for an hour or so. They had brought me so many packages that someone had to get permission to come with a wheelbarrow to cart them into the camp."

Peter made a good impression on the two ladies. They asked Pauline's grandfather in Ottawa to pull a few strings to achieve something that was absolutely unheard of, something that up to that moment had been unthinkable, that Peter visit them in Quebec over a weekend. It is not clear whether the grandfather's friend, Prime Minister Mackenzie King, had a hand in this, but permission was granted. Peter was allowed to proceed from Friday, October 3, to Sunday, October 5, 1941.

"I was asked to sign that I would be back by midnight on Sunday," he reported later. "At the time the place was full of rumours that we would be released soon. I was very much aware that I was sort of a test case, and that if there was trouble, if I was late coming back, for example, everyone would suffer.

"As far as money was concerned, I had a hundred-dollar bill that I had saved from Holland. I kept it hidden in my little bag. Wearing my one and only suit, I was driven to the railway station in Sherbrooke. Never having lived as a free man in an English-speaking country before, the mere experience of asking for a ticket in English was entirely new to me. It was amazing."

Pauline was at the station with her mother and aunt. There was great jubilation.

"They took me to their apartment and soon dinner was served. After dinner Pauline and I walked to a drugstore. I had a sundae, my first black and white sundae. Then we went up to the roof of her apartment house where we sat around and necked. I was surprised that her mother allowed her to be alone with me.

"On Saturday morning Pauline came into my room wearing her negligée. She did not make it easy for me but I behaved like a gentleman. She was a very precocious city child, sixteen going on twenty-one. We went out, exploring the city. I bought a dark blue suit, very much like a Bar Mitzvah suit, using thirty of my hundred dollars.

"On Sunday evening, they saw me off at the station. On arrival in Sherbrooke I hailed a taxi. 'To the internment camp,' I said to the driver, very much aware of the bizarre nature of the situation. I arrived early, just after ten o'clock, but the lights had already been turned off.

"It was incredible. Everybody came rushing out of their bunks. They shoved me onto a top bunk and shouted 'Speak!'"

Salivating collectively, they demanded graphic details.

"Not a single person believed me when I told them the truth."

A few months later Peter was released. He visited Pauline several times. But theirs was a variety of romance that required a barbed wire between the partners.

CHAPTER 31

The Summit

I OWE MY RELEASE TO OSCAR WILDE.

The Dublin-born Sir Edward Carson (1854–1935), later Lord Carson of Duncairn, had his first success at the English bar in a libel action brought against Oscar Wilde in 1895 by the Marquess of Queensberry. It made him England's most famous advocate. If he had fluffed the case and been forced back into Irish obscurity, he would not have been able to send Edward (born in 1920), the son of his second marriage, to Cambridge. Edward became a friend of Hans Netter, whom I saw frequently when I was a student at St. John's. Hans was the son of Cecile, a cousin of my stepfather Emil Netter.

In the late summer of 1941, my mother had asked all her friends and acquaintances whether they knew anybody in Canada who might be persuaded to sponsor me. Cecile put the question to Lady Carson, the mother of Hans's friend, who happen to know Gerald and Phyllis Birks in Montreal. Gerald was the son of Henry Birks, the founder of Canada's most prestigious jewellery firm. Cecile wrote to them, mentioning that I was the grandson of Robert Koch, the Birks of Frankfurt. Yes, of course, they wrote back, they would be pleased to follow this up.

On Monday, October 27, the commandant summoned me. Once again, I feared something terrible, and once again there was no need. I was told two people were waiting to see me in the visitors' hut. I had received no advance notice. My mother had written to me about Lady Carson's promise to ask her friends in Montreal, but I did not know whether she had heard back from them.

Awaiting me in the visitors' hut was a pleasant-looking couple. Gerald Birks was a dignified, kind gentleman in his early seventies; his handsome wife was much younger and smartly dressed. From the casual way Birks dismissed the guard, it was evident that he was a retired, high-ranking military man. I found out later that at the end of the First World War he had held the rank of lieutenant colonel.

"Well," Phyllis Birks asked, "how are they treating you?"

"Not bad," I smiled.

"How about the camp school?" the colonel asked.

"It's great." It turned out that as head of the YMCA in Montreal he knew a great deal about it from his friend, the prominent educator H.M. Tory, with whom he had worked during the war organizing the Khaki University, which had been set up by the Canadian Army in Britain to help Canadian soldiers awaiting repatriation to return to civilian life. Dr. Tory, the former president of the University of Alberta and of the National Research Council, had been to Sherbrooke. He was among those who helped to establish a relationship with the registrar of McGill University.

"Well, now," the colonel said, "I think we should get you out in the students' category. How old are you?"

"Twenty-two," I sighed. That was a year older than the age limit for students.

"I think we can fix that. I understand you're prepared to enlist?"

I swallowed hard.

"Yes, sir."

"Once you're out as a student," he continued, "I think I can get you into a decent regiment."

He asked a few more questions and then, as they were leaving, Mrs. Birks said they hoped I would stay with them in Montreal until I started university.

On Sunday afternoon, November 9, I was called out again. This time it was an immigration officer who wanted to ask me a few questions. He was a nice man. He did not mention the age limit. But he raised another obstacle.

"I understand you already have a degree." Cambridge had awarded me a bachelor of arts, even though I had been interned three weeks before the final exam. My tutor had sent me a letter when I was still in the camp, stating that had I been able to take the exam I would have had a fair chance to obtain a first-class degree. "Why would you want to get another?"

"It's the only way I can think of to get out of here," I confessed. "Anyway, wouldn't it increase my chances of getting a good civilian job to help the war effort?"

"It might."

"I understand the law school at the University of Toronto has an interesting postgraduate program."

"So," he nodded, "you've looked into that already."

He stamped a paper and scribbled something on it.

I was far from the first internee to be released from Sherbrooke. I had already attended a number of farewell parties for others who had found sponsors, usually through helpful organizations. One, Kurt Swinton, an electrical engineer, had got out as early as February. His mother was in Vancouver, and he was sponsored by a former premier of Ontario. Kurt enlisted right away, which ex-internees were not allowed to do at the time. But Kurt was an exceptional case since he had exceptionally good connections. By October he was a second lieutenant in the Royal Canadian Signal Corps and made a great splash visiting his old friends in our sister camp in Farnham, in uniform, compelling the sergeant major to salute him.

Now it was my turn. At the party given in my honour I promised to do all I could to find sponsors for my friends.

On the morning of November 10, the morning after the interview with the immigration officer, I exchanged my POW uniform for the clothes I had worn in Cambridge eighteen months earlier. A guard took me by truck to the Sherbrooke station with two others, whom I hardly knew. It was the first time we had left the camp since our dramatic arrival.

I was free.

I had imagined the train trip and my arrival in Montreal for weeks, but now that it was happening I had to remind myself again and again that I was not hallucinating.

Colonel and Mrs. Birks were at Windsor Station to pick me up. The driver took my suitcase. Their mansion was on top of the mountain, on Summit Drive, in Westmount. It had a marvellous view—Montreal lay at our feet. The driver was also the valet. He had special instructions to make me comfortable in my suite on the second floor.

It was not difficult to make a man comfortable who, the previous night, had occupied the lower half of a bunk bed in a hall shared with eight hundred others.

In due course, Colonel and Mrs. Birks received me in their living room. It was dominated by a statue of Buddha. The colonel poured me a scotch. Not in my wildest dreams had I tasted a drink as good as this.

"We have two adopted sons, Otto," Mrs. Birks said. "They call us Captain and Mate. You must do the same."

I looked puzzled.

"You see," the colonel explained, "that's what we are called on our yacht, Captain and Mate."

"Oh," I laughed. "I'll try. I'm not sure it'll come naturally to me."

"I'm sure it will after a while," Mrs. Birks smiled. "In the meantime, my learned sister will study you."

She explained that her sister, Aileen Ross, was a professor of sociology at McGill and had written her dissertation on English society in Montreal. She was trained to observe people closely.

"Now, look here," the colonel said. "Otto is a terrible name. There's a war on. You can't call yourself Otto in Canada, in wartime. Don't you have another name?"

I explained that when I was born I was named Erich. When I was three months old, my father died. His name was Otto. So I was named Otto after him.

The colonel was delighted.

"So you're saying you were called Erich at birth?"

"That's right."

"I imagine it's spelled the German way. We'll drop the 'h' and launch you as Eric Koch. That's all there is to it."

"Goodbye, Otto," Mrs. Birks beamed. "Hello, Eric."

CHAPTER 32

One Toe in Canada

THE OUTWARD CIRCUMSTANCES OF MY LIFE COULD not have changed more dramatically—even my name had changed—but I continued to suffer from a lingering form of internitis. I had expected to be cured of that pathological condition once the internment camp's gate closed behind me, but it continued for many months afterwards, just as I remained—however satisfying my new life—a refugee. On the surface, the transition from being an unhappy internee to being a happy law student at the University of Toronto was remarkably smooth. But inside nothing had really changed.

The few days I spent in the Birks residence on top of the mountain in Montreal were a fairy tale. The colonel and his wife did everything they could to make me feel at home, although I never managed to call them Captain and Mate, and I never saw them again after I left. I did make friends with Mrs. Birks's sister, Aileen Ross, with whom I kept in touch for many years. Fortunately, there was never any need for the Birks family to subsidize me. Somehow, Margo found enough money to finance my first few months in Canada until I made enough money to support myself. I do not know how she did it.

Of course, I thought that the idea of changing my name from Otto to Eric was absurd. But somehow it stuck. No Canadian knew me as Otto. And after a few months even my mother and my two siblings accepted it. That was truly extraordinary and can only be explained by our family's firm determination to leave the old world behind us.

I was far from displeased that Colonel Birks failed to place me in a good regiment. Ex-internees could not join the Canadian army until 1944, when Canada suffered serious casualties and required new recruits. As soon as it was possible, on April 28, 1944, I took the streetcar to the recruiting office at Toronto's Exhibition grounds and tried to enlist. I passed all the tests but was rejected on medical grounds. For some reason, most surprisingly, the military doctor did not like my feet. I did not protest. Eventually, as far as I know, none of the ex-internees who joined the army was sent overseas before the end of the war, either because the authorities thought they should not be exposed to the danger of the Germans capturing them or because they did not trust them. Those of us who returned to England

and joined the Pioneer Corps were allowed to join the regular army after changing their names. Many of them participated in the fighting.

Nevertheless, I did have a pseudo-military career in Canada. While at the University of Toronto from 1942 to 1943, I served in the Canadian Officers Training Corps (COTC) and was drilled once a week. As an enemy alien, however friendly, I had to report to the Royal Canadian Mounted Police on Victoria Street once a month. I occasionally put on my Canadian uniform, which always amused the police. In the summer of 1943, a few of us alumni from the internment camps were among the students who spent seven days on the drilling grounds at Niagara-on-the-Lake.

The university was pure joy. The Dean of Law accepted me after the beginning of term without hesitation on the strength of the Cambridge degree that I had received. One of my professors was Bora Laskin, who later became chief justice of Canada and whose lectures on constitutional law I enjoyed. But my enthusiasm for legal studies was limited. I seemed to have taken Lieutenant Colonel Fordham's advice seriously and decided that lawyers were not needed in wartime. I did not even try to imagine what a law degree could do for me. Therefore, I spent my time having a lively social life. I resided for some weeks in a students' cooperative on Admiral Road, and the rest of the time in various boarding houses studying the manners and mores of Finnish and Icelandic landladies.

In June 1943, I received the degree of LLB from the venerable chancellor, Sir William Mulock, who had been postmaster general in Sir Wilfrid Laurier's cabinet from 1896 to 1905.

I became part of Canadian history.

CHAPTER 33

Marriage: A Transatlantic Fantasy

DARIA WAS WORKING IN A FIRE STATION ON THE Edgware Road in March 1942 when she wrote the first letter I received from her after my release. Surprisingly, my romantic feelings towards her had continued. In a letter to her I even played with the idea of marriage. Since she was in No Man's Land, as I was, she mentioned being uprooted by the war. Her response was certainly more serious than playful.

> *March 28, 1942*
> Perfidious young man. Fickle as I know the affections of all bi-peds to be and that they have this in common with birds who fly away and hop about and are altogether unstable and erratic. I was not in the least surprised to hear no more from you. However, a letter, a most welcome letter, has now arrived.

Certainly I will marry you. Could you not cultivate the healthy practice of going barefoot as I rather
shirk the idea of the socks? As for the curtains, I
would like them to be poppy-coloured. We would
then have cushions and chair covers to match and a
very expensive wallpaper with Chinese horses on it.
I am rather a good cook, which is my chief domestic virtue and if in Canada one still eats eggs as if
they were a quite common diet we could live on
omelettes and spaghetti. I shall have to come over
in a crate marked "oranges" as I can see no possible
alternative method of transport. Certainly it would
not do to go as a human being; one would be found
out immediately and sent to prison.

I cannot pretend that I care in the least for the
Fire Service. I do not love human nature. Horses
are very beautiful outside in the fields, but at close
quarters often rather alarming. So with human
beings. Not all human beings by any means, but
a fair number.

The Lilliputian attitude to life is most evident
whenever there is officialdom. It really brings out a
most grotesque side of human beings. The idea that
one could soberly contemplate decorating people
with stripes as if they were zebras is fantastic. You
are unfortunately right.

The monotony and stupidity of school is recurring throughout life. Again, I have to wear a hat. For refusing to wear a hat at school I was perpetually subject to some form or other of mild punishment. In the end I wore them down. They allowed me to wander about in my unshielded hair.

It is hard not to give way to the prevalent feeling of the purposelessness of life. The war has torn and broken and crumbled everything away and so far has not given promise of new things to replace the old. As one cannot see an end, everything one undertakes is apt to seem aimless and futile. We have been uprooted before we began truly to develop and that makes it a thousand times harder to believe in the consistency of development. We must weather this storm and must not allow ourselves to be shattered by the wind.

I would really very much like to be married to you and think we should probably be content, as far as one can hope for contentment. I feel that we have so much in common that matters. Personally, I would like to have children as I see myself being a centre of importance as the matriarch of a vast family, all brought up à la Freud and vastly eccentric. I sympathise with your difficulties as regards "girls" and am glad that none of them come up to scratch.

However, as I am so far from you as the North Pole,
I would be glad, though jealous, if you would find
a next best person, forgive me for putting myself
first, to share your happiness and unhappiness and
darn your much-worn socks for you.

Six months later my amorous feelings towards her had by
no means abated, but this did not prevent me from mentioning to her girls whose company I was enjoying and the
excellent cellist Joyce Sands, in whose house I participated
in evenings of chamber music. She was at least ten years
older than I. Daria's next letter was highly emotional and
even included a passage about the possibility of her not
surviving the war.

September 20, 1942
O, I do love you. I am glad you feel monogamously
towards me. I do believe in monogamy. Sex is the
one biological function about which one can assert
one's independence, that is to say over which one
can deliberate, therefore one can create so much
more in it than sex itself.

Harmony between two living beings is so rare
and must be constructed with patience. I cannot

really understand the "promiscuous" school of thought.

Perhaps you will explain it to me one day.

Would it be disastrous for you to come over here now? I am too heavily implicated, for many reasons I cannot mention, even to think of getting to Canada. Apart from which, however great my tie with you, I could not leave war behind me before I had even taken the greatest risks. With such an overburdened conscience I would be a rotten companion. I feel very strongly that if you do not come now, we shall not have any opportunity of meeting again. If you look at the international situation I think you will understand why.

As a matter of fact, I doubt very much that I personally shall outlive this winter, which rather annoys me and at times makes me over sentimental. I don't want death to spoke my wheel before it has begun seriously to revolve. However, you see, I can't disguise from you and from myself that this dispatch riding is going to be a tough proposition. *Tout ce que vous vivez maintenant*, I say to myself after a wet weather ride around Hyde Park, *c'est du superflu!* This was said to a friend of mine by a French peasant who rescued him from a crashed aeroplane. By the way, it is only because you are you that I permit myself the luxury of my own possible demise. In any case, I am always anticipating it. I will probably live till eighty-five and die of common snake-bite or a surfeit of gooseberries.

I had to undertake dispatch riding because it was the most dangerous. Being the most dangerous commands the most respect.

Necessary to command respect for propagandist reasons. Also, because it cultivates in me a sense of responsibility (i.e., said respect). But as for heroism. Ugh! I loathe heroism. I deplore the return to the ancient heroic virtues, the muscular virtues, the bulldog, plum pudding virtues which our times exact. I also undertook dispatch driving because it makes me feel superior, is pleasant on fine days and leaves me free to indulge my streak of exhibitionism without *peur* or *reproche*. Hooray!

As to Herr Freud, *Ach du lieber Freud*. Your theories I avoid. *Ich liebe all my little Schmerz*. But take them very much to *Herz*. Nor do I greatly want to know. That they are due to libido.

Darling, must you live in Canada with beautiful women cellists who are safely removed from you by virtue of age, that untrustworthy sinecure of nothing at all. I can only remark that men who are old enough to be my father generally have a very incestuous approach to life. I'm sure I could support you by writing articles, at any rate for a time.

I have become a member of a certain organization. I expect you will guess what. It has been rather like climbing Mount Everest in order to get a better perspective of Primrose Hill. However, I don't regret that. At the moment I look upon it as a wise and necessary step in tune with events. My tongue is always in my cheek, where I intend it to remain, and I always remember that it is necessary to preserve in oneself a certain independence from the external world, that is to say not to lean too heavily upon any movement or idea. In other words, to give one's support, but not to be supported. The tone of my letters to you will probably change for a time because I am certain to be carried away by the first rush of enthusiasm. 'Tis the nature of the creature. Please act to some extent as a check.

Send me your love. I shall need it. I also send you mine.

Ten months went by without a letter. By the time the next one arrived I had graduated and Daria had had a love affair. It speaks volumes for our relationship that she told me about it without any inhibitions and that I was not at all upset. The romantic phase was over. I had recovered from internitis.

July 8, 1943

I feel not so much guilty as panic stricken to have sanctioned the lapse of our correspondence particularly as you are one of only three people with whom I have true conversation.

I can give you as many explanations as you wish. That I am a very busy person, and that for months past I have had little time to think, yes to think. I have been plunged into a sea of activity, in fact I have been very nearly drowned. Then also, though somehow it sounds very rude and unripe put in this way, after a six months' silence, I had a love affair and that rather obscured you for a short period. Also our correspondence has always been unsatisfactory in the sense of being so fitful and sporadic that it was like an interrupted conversation in which one loses the sense of what has gone before and becomes angry with trying to grasp one's own vanished insights.

If we start again from here, do write more often and consecutively.

Now I am taking my holidays in the Welsh hills, and I have leisure to survey all that has taken place "in the flat land."

Politically I am still in the throes of learning my practical ABC and very hard work it is. From here all that seems remote. The task of organising people in the Fire Brigades Union which absorbs my entire energy, will and intelligence normally, has no significance at the moment. In fact, I am thinking of wandering around the mountains with recruiting forms asking the inquisitive sheep to sign on the dotted line. The routine of politics I find extremely tiresome and dreary, and it is only by bearing the aim and end in mind that I can endure it. What I individually hate is reproducing a torrent of other people's thoughts (i.e., selling the British Communist Party to potential members) putting the ideas of others into action. What sustains me is the conviction that it was slowly gaining towards our objective, that there is a more and more perceptible awakening among "the people" to the need of socialism, that my day to day contacts, experiences, conversations corroborate the truth and clarity of Marxist preaching.

The right people will, of course, never be in power, but the wrong people will be less and less effective as their control over the machine becomes more and more subject to mass authority. Mass authority I mean in the practical daily needs of life. I shall always be a little lost among the contradictions of my own nature, and it is not easy to say to you, as I should like, there is one road—communism. Alas, I am still a quarter communist and three quarters Daria Hambourg. I am, only imagine, a delegate to the London Trades Council. An accredited union representative. O I am so august, so sober, so eminently sensible. But for how long? *Que diable suis-je allée faire dans cette galère?* You see, I can't write sense in Wales. I think I have been bitten by a mad horsefly.

Sitting on a mountain looking down towards the sea this evening, I had the brilliant idea that you and I should buy a ranch in Canada. (£50 war credits are due to me if I ever see them.) I would write, cook, ride and flirt with the local cowpunchers. You would farm and play the fiddle. We should invite all the natives to heated philosophical argument on Sunday afternoons. Our children (four) would be that mixture of artistic toughness which produces Hemingways and Diego Riveras. Your mother would live with us and help with the education of the children and prevent us from degenerating.

It is dark. I cannot see the paper. There are three mice enjoying themselves under my bed. To think that one crumb could be the excuse of so much innocent pleasure.

Write, write, write. Be very rude, but say you have forgiven my silence.

CHAPTER 34

The Summer of 1943

IN THE SPRING OF 1943 I WOULD HAVE JOINED MY fellow graduates and proceeded to Osgoode Hall in order to be called to the bar, however limited my interest in a legal career, had Osgoode Hall been open to "enemy aliens."

Instead, for a year and a half I summarized legal decisions for *The Canadian Abridgement*. I owed the job to one of my professors. I received fifty cents a case—whether it was a simple one line or an abridgement requiring several pages.

In order to see whether there might be more useful work for me in Ottawa, I spent several weeks during the summer writing up cases in the library of the Supreme Court. I became a great expert in topics beginning with the letters R and P. Rape was less profitable than pleading.

While I was in Ottawa I offered my services to Davidson Dunton, the chair of the War Information Board, later chair of the CBC, and to John Grierson, the unorthodox head of the new National Film Board. Grierson was assembling a staff of young people. My interview with him was memorable. He asked me only one question, whether I liked strawberries. I told him that Queen Victoria's daughter—the Kaiser's estranged mother—had introduced English strawberries to Kronberg, her final residence, in exile from her son's Berlin. Her castle was next door to my grandmother's house. No other job applicant could have done better. He would have liked to hire me, but the Civil Service Commission would not let him. A few weeks later, the regulations were changed and it would have been possible. I was disappointed when I did not get the job, but not heartbroken. It seemed too good to be true.

The weeks I spent in wartime Ottawa were invaluable in the process of my Canadianization. I particularly enjoyed the lunches I spent in the cafeteria of the Château Laurier, watching cabinet ministers lining up like everybody else—unimaginable in Europe.

But no job materialized. The idea of proceeding to S and T for *The Canadian Abridgement* left me lukewarm. Somebody told me that private schools needed replacements since so many teachers had left to serve overseas. So one day I put on my old Cranbrookian school tie, subdued my German accent, and went to see the Reverend John Bell, the headmaster of Appleby College in Oakville,

west of Toronto. He needed a French teacher. I confessed
that my French was only high-school level and that I was
useless at games. It did not matter. Nor did it matter that
I was only just twenty-four. He hired me on the spot. I
was given a little apartment on the school grounds. After
Christmas I was joined by a pleasant, well-educated young
man who was hired to teach English and games. We made
friends immediately. We went for walks after dinner and
occasionally picked up apples from the snowy grounds of
neighbouring orchards.

One evening the police arrived and arrested him. Of
course, I thought his crime was stealing apples and expected
a knock at my door. But no, he turned out to be a jewel
thief long wanted by the police, a public-spirited Robin
Hood who stole from the rich to give to the poor.

I thoroughly enjoyed teaching, much more than I had
expected. I admit I had some discipline problems with
rebellious boys in the middle grades. I threw one of them
out of my classroom because he threw spit balls at me. He
happened to be the son of the Nobel laureate Sir Frederick
Banting, the discoverer of insulin, who had died two years
earlier. Bill's mother, Lady Banting, may have complained
to the headmaster. That could have been one reason why I
was fired soon afterwards, in the middle of my second term.
There were other reasons that were never clearly spelled
out, such as my discipline problems, and my having told

another teacher that, remembering my happy experience in Cranbrook, I was planning to contact the local girls school to join forces for exercises in French conversation. He was horrified and may have told the headmaster about it.

Mr. Bell fired me in style. He said I did not fit into the school. He asked me what I was going to do, now that I was unemployed. I told him not to worry, I would do war work in a factory. He thought that was a bad idea and, in my presence, called a member of his board, the president of Toronto Elevators—grain elevators at the foot of Spadina Avenue in Toronto—and told him that I was the best man on his staff but unfortunately I was "the classical type" and did not fit in. The man agreed to take me on as a favour to Mr. Bell, but it turned out he had no use for a classical type either and never bothered to try me out.

Twenty years later, when I was at the CBC in Toronto, Bill Banting called me and asked me whether I remembered him. I said of course, how could I forget? Another question followed: did I have a job for him as a television producer? It so happened that there was a vacancy. I knew he was gifted and hired him. He did very well for many years.

I was still teaching at Appleby College when this letter from Daria arrived. There were no more references, playful or otherwise, to a future marriage.

October 2, 1943

These long silences are unintentional. I have no idea of allowing our exchange of letters to discontinue, or of allowing our Huxleyan relationship to lapse.

I love hearing from you. Particularly when you are disconsolate and need my moral support. Here at least I feel is an excuse and invitation for my earthly presence. I am delighted to fulfill the important role of link between two continents. Yet I fear you glean from me a truer insight into the soul of Daria than [into] the social structure of Great Britain. And I must confess that you are more interesting than America.

I have written several times to you but in moods of such cynical and suicidal despair that I destroyed my letters. We should encourage one another's hope, not confirm one another's pessimism.

I find my environment so uncongenial in point of view of company rather than anything else, that the hysterics of war and apprehension of the future prey on my nerves sometimes to an unendurable extent. There is something about the repressed and cultureless social pattern of middle-class life which sinks me into abysmal gloom. My present background is a training college for women and I live with a female staff of about twenty.

A rather dreary form of Lesbianism is well in evidence. Apart from that, the atmosphere is genteel boarding school. To talk about anything other than banality or bawd is bad form old bean. And we make each other apple-pie beds at night which is hysterically funny. Ha ha.

The political situation is far from heartening. Also I feel a growing impotence to deal with it. There is the usual fatal conflict between my knowledge of what must be done and my disinclination to undertake it. I clearly see the need for socialism, the imminent danger of Fascism. I detest the necessary means for convincing and enlisting the people. I detest political activity. I cannot hide from myself the consciousness of what a people's Britain on Marxist-Leninist-Stalinist lines will produce in the way of art. Or the interference with the artist which state control will mean. I also cannot hide from myself that Socialism is the logical next step in the direction of progress. I am not a sufficiently developed artist to achieve the difficult synthesis between art and propaganda at this stage. Political activity is such an effort to me that it drains me of creative energy for my own work. The pressure of conscience and awareness of danger says act.

The natural being reacts from a path of practice foreign to its inherent laws. And the outcome is that I can neither write nor tub-thump. So you must excuse a note of gloom and restlessness.

I am relieved that the problem of a dull job has solved itself. Some people can succeed very well in dividing themselves into watertight compartments and can endure a dull daily grind and yet enjoy the residue of their lives. I cannot. Dull jobs exhaust me with pulling against the yoke and leave me at six p.m. with a huge feeling of distaste and boredom. The experience is one to be avoided.

I hope you will allow your pupils every latitude to express themselves. Encourage them to revolt against discipline. Encourage them to lie, steal and commit adultery as soon as possible so that they may realize the monotony of conventional sin and not waste time in pursuing it later on. I long to hear an account of your experiences.

I congratulate all of us and God on your mother's departure.[‡] A cheering and consoling example that there is some divine if wayward and spasmodic justice somewhere which recognizes and rewards

---

‡   My mother had at last succeeded in arranging a crossing in a convoy to New York.

human greatness. If ever in the future I feel inclined to weep over my misfortunes, I will remember the stoic courage and constructiveness of your mother and content myself with spitting in fate's blind eye.

This is an unsatisfactory answer to your insistent cry for more articulation. But I will soon write again.

The intellectual in a boys' school should invariably become a pervert. It is *de rigueur*. Let me know whether this happens to you, as I should be intrigued, though disapproving.

I daresay you will soon forget me in the arms of a charming young Canadian girl. Then you will compose me a difficult and embarrassing letter explaining how your relationship with me was ever of the most insubstantial nature and you hoped I never imagined, etc., etc.

Five weeks later Daria wrote to me again. I was still at Appleby College when I received it.

November 11, 1943
What about correspondence, you hypocrite? Make me no protestations, I'll have none of them.

This is a statement of my spiritual accounts to date.

Political. Slowly losing interest. With my increasing admiration for the work of the Communist Party goes an increasing reluctance to undertake it. The following analysis will show you why. My aesthetic ideals are that the routine of life should be graceful. Buildings, clothes, eating utensils, toys, every necessary and superfluous object should please aesthetically. This is impossible because materials, craftsmanship and time cannot be had in sufficient quantity for our crowded civilisation. It is also improbable because individual taste has been so corrupted by mass exigency. The innocent eye has been clouded with ammonia and bleary vision is likely to be in evidence for some few generations to come. Perhaps the greatest irony is for me that the CP, which could achieve the least unsatisfactory solution to this problem by planning production and experimenting with design without too much fear of ruin, will fail to do so because the people will be the sole consumers and therefore dictators of taste. Without searching for causes, I have no illusions about the taste of the people as such. Among other obstacles it is interesting to observe that re-education in taste will mean re-education in emotional disassociation. Here I talk undiluted rubbish. What I mean is nothing is seen for what it is, but all is camouflaged in association. A vase of unspeakable ugliness is treasured because it was a birthday present from some sacred memory. And then again my own taste is so unformed. I feel I could devote my life quite easily to re-educating myself.

I do not therefore expect to see the face of civilisation, or should I not say, its ugly mug transformed by any mass political movement.

My humanitarian ideals are that too much suffering should be reduced to suffering. Poverty and unthinking tyranny are two huge factors in too much suffering which could be dispensed with by socialism.

However, I am not blind to the realisation that seizure of power will involve the utmost cruelty to the deposed class. That knowledge, involved as I am emotionally with that class and individuals within it, halts my impetus. And then I know people and their petty spites too well to be optimistic about the process of revolution. I can tell to a certain extent how grim it will be by the measure of the obstacles which I meet with, humanly speaking, in carrying out Party work now. Alas, by the nature of Party propaganda which is directed by the nature of its consumers.

All these objections of mine rob me of the vital strength, patience, endurance and faith which are indispensable to a political worker, and thrice indispensable to a middle-class supporter of CP activity. They do not rob me of conviction as the absolute necessity and rightness of socialist revolution in view of the industrial character of our civilisation.

I can see that living through the process of transmutation will exact the utmost philosophical fortitude and cunning.

Continuing the accounts, Freud comes next in order of precedence. Marx and Freud, these are the dominant figures for our generation to reckon with. Libido, libido, ruddy old libido, sang a character in a book. By what balance is one to weigh the pros and cons of psychoanalysis?

I have never understood the parent substitute theory. If it be true that men and women marry an Oedipean partner, why is it that such marriages are successful? And what about marriages which are not founded on the residue of an Oedipus complex? And so much is glossed over by that morbid science of the fullness of life. And so many details are overlooked in the attempt to make theory embrace the whole of human life in all its intricacy. And the idea of treatment. What an impertinent ascendancy that of the analyst over the patient. And to look upon falling in love as a scientific progression towards positive transference! And allowing the theory to be ninety percent valid. There remains the delicate technical question of application. I cannot believe that in such an intimate context there can be no personal relationship between analyst and analysand. And admitting this, what risk attends the prospect of genuine result from such a synthetic venture. Again a tremendous gulf of personality may separate analyst and analysand, a gulf of understanding and outlook which, in view of the importance of personal contact between the two, cannot be bridged over simply by a body of abstract scientific knowledge. I conclude that the science of psychology is still very underdeveloped and shows all the self-conceit of the immature. I would like to know your views on the question.

Has your mother arrived in America yet? Please give me news of her when you write.

I am reading *The Kierkegaard Journals* again, some history, of which I know nothing except that King Alfred burned the castles, Lady Jane Grey was executed at sixteen, Charles II apologised for being "such an unconscionable time a-dying" and Queen Victoria was "not amused" by smutty stories, and

a History of Architecture. I only pray, and so must you, that I shall persist in quenching this sudden thirst for knowledge...

My love to you, dear schoolmaster,

Daria

This was the last letter I received from Daria.

CHAPTER 35

Nine Toes in Canada

I WAS RELEASED FROM CAMP N IN SHERBROOKE ON November 10, 1941. The Japanese attacked Pearl Harbor on December 7. Robert joined the American Army right away. All I could do for "the war effort" was to allow the Canadian army to drill me once a week, as a member of the COTC on the campus of the University of Toronto and for seven days at Niagara-on-the-Lake in the summer of 1943.

After the abruptly terminated episode as French teacher and three weeks' non-experience in the grain trade, I tried my luck in journalism. This time I succeeded beyond all expectations. I made my adventure with the engaging new English teacher and public-spirited jewel thief the subject of a short story and offered it to B.K. Sandwell, the editor of *Saturday Night* magazine. He was one of the enlightened Canadian intellectuals who had grasped the absurdity of keeping refugees from Germany and Austria behind barbed wire and had written about it. So he understood my background. Sandwell had wide experience as an academic and editor. In 1919 he and Stephen Leacock had been colleagues as associate professors of economics at McGill. Not only did he accept my story right away, but he also asked me to write articles and stories for the magazine, and amusing little items for the weekly column The Passing Show. The longer pieces were to appear under my name and pseudonyms for twenty-five dollars a week. I was delighted. Through the summer and fall of 1944 I wrote articles on a wide variety of subjects, such as "The Allies' First Line Is the Underground" (June 11, 1944) and "The Transferable Vote" (September 30, 1944), and "What Keeps the Zombies from Going Active" (November 25, 1944), a reflection on the conscription crisis in Quebec. In one article I wrongly predicted that there would be not much immigration from Europe to Canada after the war since all available manpower would be required for rebuilding a shattered continent. I did pieces on the novelist Morley Callaghan and the CBC drama producer Andrew Allan, the mastermind of the compelling Sunday night radio plays *Stage 44*.

I did not get my chance to "do my bit" for the war effort until December 1944, when the CBC hired me to join the new International Service—later Radio Canada International—"The Voice of Canada"—to broadcast on shortwave to Germany twice a day from Montreal. Our broadcasts were to be conducted as psychological warfare in line with those of the BBC and the Voice of America, and under the policy guidance of the Department of External Affairs. First there were test transmissions, before the official opening by Mackenzie King in February 1945.

No job could have been better suited to ease my conscience. At last I would be able to contribute without having to kill anybody and without being in any danger of being killed. It was perfectly designed to lubricate my transition from No Man's Land to the joys of being Canadian.

I learned much that was to prove useful later. At first, the German section consisted of two camp alumni, Helmut Blume, an ardent Berliner, and myself. It was Blume who had hired me. He was a concert pianist, five years older than I, a friend until his death in 1998. His German was considerably better than mine. He was twenty-four when he left Germany. I was fifteen. He put great emphasis on style and accuracy. Neither of us had ever written a newscast in German, but he found it easier than I did. We produced and delivered two broadcasts a day, one at seven in the morning—lunchtime in Germany—and the other at one. Later two other ex-internees joined us, Edgar Sarton and Franz Kraemer. In 1946 Blume left to teach at McGill—he went on to become Dean of Music—and I succeeded him as head of the section. By 1950 I was also responsible for broadcasts to Austria and Italy. In 1953 I was transferred to Toronto to become program organizer in the Department of Talks and Public Affairs. Later I assumed other positions in Toronto and Montreal. Blume continued to make regular contributions on a freelance basis. He also became an excellent broadcaster on musical subjects in English.

We avoided the word "propaganda" to describe our work: that was Dr. Goebbels's word. But of course we were propagandists. I often boast that I was the most effective broadcaster in the entire history of the CBC. I told the Germans to put down their arms. They listened and they did.

We told ourselves that our job was not to make propaganda but to present information about Canada and commentaries on the news in a Canadian perspective. That is what we did. We received highly classified directives from the Department of External Affairs, which usually corresponded with our own ideas. Fifty years later, the social scientist Arthur Siegel wrote a history of the early years of the CBC's International Service based mainly on material in the Ottawa archives. He discovered that, in terms of content and policy, our broadcasts were considered exemplary. It is regrettable that none of our scripts survived.

We certainly took our work seriously. But we had to wait until years after the end of the war to receive evidence that some Germans actually listened to us. Of course, during the war, listening to shortwave broadcasts was strictly forbidden. If a radio was tuned to an enemy station, even if it was turned off, and was seen by a loyal Nazi, let alone by the Gestapo, it was *prima facie* evidence of guilt. After the war we received mail and answered some of it on the air. In the late 1950s, a German immigrant visited me in my CBC office in Toronto and presented me with a bottle of scotch. He said he had been a regular listener, remembered my voice and my name, and wanted to express his gratitude. Too bad this only happened once.

Soon the BBC and the Voice of America began to relay weekly shows that we provided. In 1946 we established direct relations with newly licensed German radio stations and sent to them programs on disc for their school broadcasts.

Thirty-five thousand German prisoners of war had been sent to camps in Canada, some housed in camps considerably larger than those we interned civilians had occupied from 1940 to 1943. These were now the homes of real prisoners of war, not refugees. We visited them regularly and recorded messages and talks and discussions, even concerts, on large equipment brought in on trucks—tape had not yet become available—and found this material an invaluable enrichment for our broadcasts. In the postwar years, re-education had taken the place of psychological warfare as one of our purposes, and we found, with the help of Canadian intelligence officers, a number of anti-Nazi prisoners to assist us.

The years I spent in the International Service were hugely important in my life. They prepared me for a satisfying career in the CBC, both in radio and television. I formed lasting friendships with many colleagues in the other language sections, and I got to know the country. I was among the broadcasters who covered the royal tour in 1951. When we said goodbye to Princess Elizabeth and Prince Philip in Portugal Cove, Newfoundland, a picture was taken of René Lévesque and me waving the Union Jack. Unfortunately, I have lost it. For a few months Lévesque worked for the French Section.

In 1948 there was the Berlin Airlift and the Cold War broke out. Germany was divided. We were, of course, broadcasting both to the west and to the east. Our work became complicated. Grave policy questions arose as anti-communism became part of re-education. And what about Tito who, in 1948, broke with Stalin? Our boss, Jean Dési, a former ambassador to Brazil, a stronger anti-communist than his superiors in Ottawa, did not agree with their directive to back Tito, the lesser evil. Tito remained a communist, didn't he? He countermanded the directive. This kind of problem became particularly troublesome in the McCarthy years in the early 1950s, when a critic accused two of our colleagues, in sections other than mine, of not being anti-communist enough, for sinister reasons. Neither was the slightest security risk. One of them was transferred to Toronto to become program director of CBLT, the new television station; the other left. Henning Sorensen, the head of our Danish Section and a professional journalist, was a true believer in communism. I did not know it at the time. He was spared because he had convinced the RCMP in the early 1940s that, despite being a communist, he was no security risk. Sorensen was allowed to join Naval Intelligence in Ottawa. He had been an assistant to Dr. Norman Bethune during the Spanish Civil War and had helped him develop the famous blood banks.

The National Film Board suffered eighteen casualties who had no way of fighting back. The board was part of the civil service. There were no unions. Nor were there any legal remedies. Those who were fired, and their friends, did not think public opinion would have been on their side if they had made a fuss about it.

It was good to live in Montreal. My French was still execrable, despite being good enough to teach to the boys at Appleby College. It was actually better than that of many Anglo-Saxons in Montreal. I had learned it in the Goethe Gymnasium in Frankfurt and refined it under an excellent French teacher in Cranbrook. But I had never lived in a French-speaking country. I made a determined effort to speak French to Quebeckers.

I was lucky that John Newmark invited me to share his apartment at 1454 Crescent Street. His French was excellent. Like Helmut Blume, John was a pianist who had been a friend in camp. He was not a solo virtuoso like Helmut but a uniquely gifted accompanist, very much in demand by world-class singers such as Kathleen Ferrier. He was also the mentor of the young Maureen Forrester.

John was a fastidious housekeeper and cook. I had to be careful where to put the dishes after washing them. His elegant living room contained a Steinway and an Emily Carr landscape he had bought from his camp friend Max Stern, the owner of the Dominion Gallery on Sherbrooke Street. Max was the first major art dealer to sell her work. He had been known in the camp as the *Kunst-Stern* (Art-Stern), to distinguish him from other Sterns.

John's living room served as a salon to which friends were often invited to listen to music and converse, often in French. Amazingly, John could sight-read the most complicated contemporary music but could not play *O Canada* from memory. In 1946 Franz Kraemer joined us. As a teenager in Vienna he had studied composition with Alban Berg, the composer of *Wozzeck* and *Lulu*. Kraemer was later to produce seventeen operas for the CBC in ten years and to receive the Order of Canada in 1981. Like John, Franz was interested in new Canadian music. After the war, with veterans returning and the Catholic Church in decline, Montreal was full of new ideas, just the right place for young adventurous artists, musicians, actors, and journalists to have a good time in John's salon.

I prospered in his basement for three years, from 1945 to 1948.

CHAPTER 36

I Have Arrived

I MARRIED SONIA MECKLENBURG ON MAY 11, 1948, five years after Daria's last letter. Since that day I have had no other wife. She has in common with Daria that she is an anti-conventional rebel against the bourgeoisie. But in all other respects she is different. She has no interest in the arts and philosophy. When asked whether she likes music she answers, "It doesn't bother me."

Sonia is robust, self-sufficient, self-reliant, undemanding, irreverent, and stubborn. She prefers to do things herself rather than accept help. She did not have a doctor until she was in her eighties and prefers her own company to that of others, immediate family excepted. She prefers the night to the day. It is almost impossible to give her presents.

Sonia met Doug Monk, the CBC International Service's personnel manager, at the tennis court and told him casually she was between jobs. She had been a typist at Sun

Life Insurance Company. He told her to come and see him in his office. She did. Doug needed typists and hired her. She started work in February 1948.

It was time for straightforward, no-nonsense earthiness. Three years in John's basement was enough. I needed to get away from High Culture. I had just split from a girlfriend with whom I had shared the basement for three months. She was perfectly satisfactory and fitted in beautifully. But in the end I found her a little pretentious. She quickly recovered and married the head of the Swedish Section. There had been a number of other girls. One of them was nice to me only because John liked to use her as his page turner. I was, as a musical friend put it, "holding auditions." None of them passed.

When I saw Sonia I was besotted. She was twenty-three and gorgeous. It was cold. She was wearing a fur coat. I did not notice that it was not, let us say, the latest style. She was driving a car. I did not notice that it was her father's and was rusty and ancient. Walter Schmolka, the head of the Czech Section, immediately pounced on her. It was not easy to outmanoeuvre him.

Sonia was told that if she married me she could not work at the CBC in the same unit as her husband. I was not prepared to leave the CBC. This was an excellent reason for marrying me since she did not like work. Another was that

I promised her that if she married me I would take her to London on our honeymoon. I did.

And I married her because I thought she would be an excellent mother. She has been to our three children.

To say that Sonia was brought up in a stable would be grossly inaccurate but not entirely wrong. There was a tight father–daughter bond. She spent as much time with him as she could. Philip Mecklenburg trained race horses and needed to encourage them on racecourses in Canada, New England, and Florida. He was a small, muscular, sentimental, restless man full of compressed energy and passionate intensity who had the face of a Russian violinist. His ethical code was mid-Victorian. He listened to the Metropolitan Opera radio broadcasts on Saturday afternoons. He called Sonia "Dimples" because she had dimples. He loved horses. When they were sick he knew what was wrong with them and sometimes actually cured them. By the time I arrived on the scene, his career was already in decline and it was rare for one of his horses to win a race.

Philip had not become involved with horses until the mid-1930s. He was an insurance man and did well until the Depression. At one time he owned an apartment building, but he lost it. He was restless and impatient. Horses had been in his background: there were horses on the estate in Lithuania his father had managed when Philip was a boy. I was told one day a friend asked him whether he would

like to train a horse. He said, why not? The rest is history.
The horse won a race. Then there were two horses. Then
three. Some he trained, some he owned.

He came to Canada from Lithuania before the First
World War, when he was in his late teens. He was a member of a large Jewish family and had several close relatives
already in North America. He had many friends, but he
had no use for his relatives. Religion played no role in his
life. He had a twin brother, Harry, with whom he did not
agree on the day of their birth because Harry used the
Jewish calendar. Soon after his arrival in Canada, Philip
went up north to look for gold—and found some. With
some partners he invested in land, on which in 1924 the
original Montreal Forum was built. When war broke out
in 1914, Philip joined the army immediately and fought in
France for four years. He rose to the rank of captain. He
was shell-shocked—it showed in his speech—but he survived. He never talked about the war. While he was away,
the city of Montreal took his land for non-payment of taxes.

In 1918, before returning to Canada, Philip spent a few
days in London where he fell in love with Dora Cave, who
became his war bride. She, too, came from a large Jewish
family—her parents had come from Poland, not Lithuania—but, unlike Philip's, it was a close, loving family,
and she remained an integral part of it all her life. And
so did Sonia and her younger sister, Marcia. Both spent

long periods of their childhood with the Caves in North London and loved their aunts, uncles, and cousins dearly. Whenever Philip won a race, he handed his wife a bundle of cash and said, "Shnooks, take the girls out of school and go home to England." That is what Dora and her daughters happily did. Their schooling did not suffer. The fact that Sonia did not go to university had nothing to do with it—she did not go to university because everybody else did. Or perhaps she was just not interested enough. Marcia was more conventional and would have liked to have gone, but at the time when money was needed to finance this the horses did not cooperate.

It took a long time before Dora got used to living in Montreal after having been snatched away from her close-knit family. She was a good pianist and, once in Montreal, performed occasionally as an accompanist. She also liked to play cards—bridge and poker—was attractive and sociable and made friends easily.

When Sonia besotted me, Philip was in Florida. I was asked to speak to him on the phone. I was nervous. So was he. Sonia had told me that since he had been fighting the Germans for four years he was not going to be pleased with a son-in-law whose father had fought on the other side. The long distance line was bad. I thought he said: "I have only two dollars." I replied, "I am not marrying your daughter for her money." But he was actually saying something quite different. He was saying, "I have only two daughters. Please look after her."

We got married in New York. We stayed in Margo and Paul's house in Forest Hills, where my mother also lived. Philip and Dora had visited my mother earlier, to establish diplomatic relations. The reason we did not marry in Montreal was that in Quebec a rabbi would have had to officiate. Sonia had no use for rabbis, and I did not care one way or another. So we married in the chambers of Mr. Justice Null in City Hall. But the marriage has been valid for sixty-seven years.

There was a small reception. Robert came with his wife, Charlotte, whom he had married a year earlier. A few old friends from Frankfurt attended.

No Man's Land soon became a distant memory.

Three Postscripts

Dinner with Daria

ON JUNE 21, 1947, HELMUT BLUME SENT ME THIS report from the Strand Palace Hotel in London. Portions of it were written in German, which I have translated.

> Mr. Eric Koch: $20.00
> for the report on
> Miss Daria Hambourg

> I phoned the lady but you had given me a number that was no good. Unfortunately, a certain Mr. Hamburger answered. To make it short, the entire boarding house got all excited until the situation was cleared up. I then called Daria at her parents' place and managed to catch her and arranged for a

rendezvous in my hotel for five o'clock the next day, spelled out my name, and gave her my room number. By ten to six she had still not arrived. I called her sister, who appears to be very nice. She said, "What a bloody shame. I think Daria is somewhat erratic. Are you sure she got your name right? Will you hold on a minute? My little child is in difficulty…" And then—silence…

Eric—did you intend to get me into such a mess?

Well, to come back to our little tragedy, Daria *had* been at the hotel, at five thirty, had got my name wrong and been given a wrong room number, well, can you blame the staff, overworked as they are, that they told her they didn't have anybody by that name staying in that room. Did you think I would give up? I did not. I phoned her again at her digs—her sister had given me the number and she had just happily arrived home. We had a very annoying little talk and I forced her to get back on the tube. At seven thirty we fell into each other's arms.

Just a second—I have to drink a glass of water.

Where were we? Ah yes—there she was, in front of my critical eyes, which, for your benefit, registered every detail. Even at the danger of upsetting your innermost feelings, I will be totally honest. Of glamour, not a trace. Her stockings had dropped.

Her shoes—model 1923. And had not been polished since. Her face untouched by sunshine, her
teeth yellowish, long, somewhat dirty fingernails,
pretty blue eyes, her voice *very* English—for some
mysterious reason I expected her to speak *refugese.*
Her manner slightly embarrassed, subdued, tense,
her laughter loud and high-pitched…Well, then we
went to have a drink, somewhere around Regent
Street, I forget where. Then we sat for an hour and
chitchatted, then we went to Soho and studied the
hookers, after which we had dinner at a small French
restaurant. (Had you written to her that I am in
Europe on an expense account, you scoundrel? It
cost me eighteen shillings. Including phone calls it
comes to more than a pound. Four dollars, fifteen
cents. In October you will pay up.)

Well, now, I did not speak about you as openly
as I am writing about her. In fact, I told her a bunch
of lies. I described you as "such a lovable fellow,
immensely popular with everybody, very talented
and successful, mature, brilliant, tall and good looking, a wonderful sense of humour and timing," and
similar bullshit. But I was very convincing. She ate
it all up. (Except that at times she let down the
shutters, withdrew for a few moments and was inac-
cessible.) She has a frustrating habit: she holds her

fingers before her mouth when she speaks, a mannerism on whose meaning you'll find all the dope in *Freud*, Volume XXXIII. Section A, An. 9, pp. 121–984. She asked me whether you were contemplating marriage. But she wasn't as blunt about it as this sounds. Besides, she didn't imply whether you were contemplating marriage with her, but just generally. I hummed and hawed, I snickered, I coughed. Of course I didn't do any of these things. I answered with a clear blue-eyed, German NO. She told me that she had had a number of jobs during the war, among them "fa-fighting"—fire-fighting to you. And now? "Oh, I'm just writing a novel." She said this without any ornamentation or elaboration, with such innocent eyes that I felt great warmth for her in my heart. She has published a little book "that nobody takes any notice of," a monograph of a British artist—I forget his name—but he designed the cover of *Punch*. She expects, or rather hopes, to finish her novel this year. Another thing she said was, "Please tell Otto that he can send me his emissaries every year or so until I am thirty, but that this method will become increasingly difficult as I approach forty." I thought that was rather good. (I must mention here that I had no idea you had sent George [Brandt, professor of drama, Bristol

University, also an ex-internee, whose report has been lost] on a similar errand just a year ago. I thought you had not known anything about her since 1922. You cad, sir!)

I struck her as very Canadian, strangely enough. She had never seen anybody looking less German. (I put that down to poetic licence on her part.) She also implied that what she had seen of Canadians she had not liked very much. I took a bow.

Well, that's about all. We parted near Piccadilly, somewhere on the whore-polluted street of the Empire. She just said, "Well, Helmut, I think I'll leave you now. And please, do forgive me that I didn't ask you to dinner, but you know my parents are rather formal and always like a little time for preparation. But do give me a ring when you come back." And then she moved off, a little figure in dark brown, without pretence, without love, but with courage, faith and beauty in her soul...

Well, forgive me, Eric, if I seem rather beastly but the truth is that I have been wondering ever since I set eyes on her what in the world made you so violently interested. Remember your note on the list of addresses? "Absolutely imperative" in red letters. Maybe I got it all wrong. Maybe I am trespassing from the bounds of an objective report into the realm of delicate privacy. But I have known bluestockings of this kind of both sexes and I have always been very impatient with them. Maybe she *will* produce a profound volume. So what? An artist does not lighten his burden by showing it off to other people. And I can't help feeling that she suffers from that trend a bit, maybe unknown to herself. Or maybe we just didn't hit it off. But even so there would remain a lack of naturalness to be accounted for, plus the very obvious disregard for the superficial things in a woman's life, like make-up and dainty dresses. Incidentally, she said that she was no good at writing letters but that she was going to send you a copy of her novel when it was published. I have a feeling that she will write to you this time...

St. John's Wood: The Sequel

In 1995, when I looked at Daria's letters again, nothing seemed more natural than to include parts of them in a book I was planning about my transition from one life to another. The first thing to do, obviously, was to find out whether Daria was still alive. If so, I calculated, she would be seventy-five. I remembered she had an older sister, Nadine, in Cambridge. I phoned her. Nadine told me that Daria had died three years previously, in January 1992, that she had converted to the Russian Orthodox faith, had had severe mental problems, and had spent the last years of her life in a community in Devonshire presided over by Father Benedict Ramsden, a priest and a psychiatrist. As to publishing her letters, Nadine referred me to her younger sister Michal in London, who was looking after family affairs and who had been close to Daria.

Daria's letters to me would be her primary literary legacy. Before 1995 I had done nothing to get them published. For one thing, I understood that they could not stand by themselves and needed a context. I could not think of one until I decided on a memoir of the five years in which I knew her. For another, I felt guilty for not having made any effort to keep in touch with her. The reason for this was my acute discomfort about the romantic phase of our correspondence. I believed I had allowed feelings that were natural in camp after a year and a half behind barbed wire to last far too long. I could not understand why this happened. Even today I am not sure I understand it. Did I pretend to myself that I liked her more than I actually did? That is not impossible. Did I feel she used me to sharpen her writing skills? Perhaps that was an element. I was sure that Daria was a born writer, and for years I kept my eyes open for reviews of books she might have written. I found none.

I remembered Daria's references in the early part of our correspondence to Michal's wedding and to the Prom concert in Albert Hall where she played Saint-Saëns' Second Piano Concerto. I phoned Michal right away. She knew immediately who I was, even though my name was no longer Otto. I told her of the purpose of my call and said that on my next trip to England in the following spring I would like to visit her.

"By all means," she said. "But please call first. My husband and I are going to Africa. But we should be back by the time you arrive."

I soon found out that this was her second husband, Ian MacPhail. Michal, having resumed her career as a concert pianist after a long absence, had established the Hope Hambourg Musical Trust, initially funded by the sale of a valuable viola that belonged to her cousin Hope. The trust offered grants to alleviate hardship. Her philanthropic activities addressed emotional issues, too, having participated in setting up a counselling service for the National Association for Gifted Children.

I phoned a few weeks before leaving for England.

"I don't want to see you," she said.

I thought I had misheard her.

But she repeated it.

"I don't mind talking to you on the phone," she said. "But I don't want to see you. When Daria needed you, you were not available. Now you need us. We are not available."

This could only mean one thing: Michal felt that I was a cad.

When I was in London I called, as Michal had suggested. She was not at home. But her husband was.

Ian MacPhail spoke to me in the tone of the sergeant major in Sherbrooke.

"Did you not hear what my wife told you? Stop pestering us. Bugger off!"

Father Benedict Ramsden

Father Benedict Ramsden was the director of the Community of St. Antony and St. Elias in Totnes, Devonshire, in which Daria had lived and died. I phoned him in 1998, but he regretfully declined to talk about her since he had been her priest and her doctor.

I emailed him in January 2014, without referring to my previous communication, to tell him about my plan to write this book. He responded.

> Thank you so much for your email. I am extremely excited that you are writing a tribute to Daria. She was, as you say, highly talented, extraordinarily

troubled and a remarkable personality. I shall look forward to your book very much.

But to turn to your "big question." I never met Sonia, Mère Marie, but you obviously know about her, so you will be aware that she and her husband, then living in France, disappeared, as far as the rest of the family were concerned, early in the Second World War. As it became more and more clear as to what was happening to people of Jewish origin who had disappeared, Daria will have lived in the expectation of disappearing herself when Hitler, as he surely would, conquered England. As things turned out he did not. It became clear that Sonia's husband had met the fate of so many Jews, but Sonia had taken refuge in the convent at Bussy-en-Othe, and had survived…

Daria lived with the remembrance of this horror for much of her later life. In her periods of depression, she sank into an expectation of her own being taken away to a concentration camp and the horrors she would meet there. This was very terrible to see; her distress was dreadful and after about a week of it, she would, in her worst periods of depression, pass into a state of catatonia. I won't distress you with a description of it.

From this state she would suddenly shoot into a state of near ecstatic mania in which she would feel intensely creative, longing to write. Here was another tragedy.

Mother Mary also suffered, as I am sure you are aware, from what is now called bipolar syndrome. It was not always easy for the convent to handle, but it was extremely creative. In the manic phase of her condition, she produced a vast amount of work translating the service books of the Orthodox church. Her work needed editing, but it was the major part of the work of these translations. As you will know, Bishop Kallistos Ware cooperated in their production, and the most important of them were published by no less a publisher than Faber, while the rest were published in a very simple form by the convent. As a result of all this, Mother Mary went on being a very creative person until very nearly the end of her life.

Tragically, this was not so for Daria. Mother Mary had lived her life in France where electroconvulsive therapy was not used as a treatment for bipolar syndrome. Daria lived in England, where it was. I am not blaming anyone for using it. Daria, faced with her depressions, would beg for ECT, but the repeated use of ECT does damage to the brain, to the memory, to the powers of concentration. Daria was so damaged that her urge to write was defeated and was in fact a source of major suffering—a frustration so terrible to her that I am confident that I am not exaggerating when I use the word "suffering."

I am sure the story of Mother Mary's survival of the Nazi occupation and her conversion to Russian Orthodoxy in the course of that survival will have played its part in Daria coming to make contact with the Russian Orthodox Church. I think, however, that the main cause of her conversion was Metropolitan Anthony Bloom, the Russian Orthodox bishop in London for many years. He was a remarkable man. Daria had a great devotion to him. It was he who referred her to this community, where she was to spend most of the last years of her life. Looking after Daria was not easy (the nuns at Bussy, who knew that Daria's condition was far more severe than Mother Mary's, used to refer to me with hushed voices as "Le Bon Père Benoît," because they could not imagine how on Earth we put up with it!). I have to tell you, though, that I regard Daria as one of my dearest friends ever, and for all its difficulties, excitements, awfulness, amazing stories, etc., etc., knowing Daria was an immensely enriching experience.

I have never forgotten how, one day, when I was feeling rather "down," but I think not showing it, Daria, standing by me, pressed two fingers into the palm of my hand, squeezed it, and said, "I know, Father dear, I know." I was, as I said, feeling rather down, and this woman, who regularly suffered periods of unutterable horror, beside which my "downness" was utterly trivial, had noticed, and offered sympathy. Trying to write it, it sounds like nothing, but I still remember it vividly.

Having told you that story, may I tell you another, which may convince you that I am just crazy, but it also has a great vividness for me. One January 15th, I celebrated the liturgy very early in the morning for the Feast of St. Paul of Thebes (according to Jerome, the first hermit ever). It was also the anniversary of Daria's death…It was a day on which I faced something really horrible, an unfolding family tragedy. As the moment in the liturgy when one sings a litany for the departed approached, I found myself not so much praying for the repose of Daria's soul, as in some way reaching out to her. I became vividly aware of two people standing beside me. On my left, St. Paul of Thebes (many scholars would say that he never existed except as a figment of Jerome's imagination writing a rather fanciful story) and, on my right, Daria. I do not mean that I saw them; I did not hear them; they were just very, very vividly there. In my diaries over the succeeding months, I mention it several times, and inevitably this rather vivid experience (I really do not have those sorts of experiences) would come to mind annually as I celebrated that liturgy on the 15th; but by about five years later, I find myself writing in my diary, that of course I felt them there. I was desperate, and the mind plays tricks to comfort one when one is desperate, and I had dismissed the whole incident in that sort of way. But then, two or three years ago I paid a visit to Egypt, and to the monastery of St. Paul of Thebes. I approached the tomb (it is really an empty cenotaph) of St. Paul, and as I was about to reverence it in the traditional way, the priest standing beside it said to me, "tell me about your vision of St. Paul." I stared at him in some surprise, and he said, "you've seen him, haven't you?" "No," I replied, "I did not see him." He reached out his hand to me and said "please tell me about it." So I did.

I really do not know what to make of all that, but I have to say that not long ago, reading an essay on the restoration of some wall paintings in that monastery and coming across the essayist's opinion that Paul did actually exist and that Jerome's account is an admittedly very fanciful story based on a real person, I noticed myself thinking, 'well, I know he exists', and if I know that he exists, I suppose I have to say, I know that Daria exists—a very remarkable person.

Yours,
Father Benedict

Final Note

IN 2014 THE HAMBOURG FAMILY GAVE ME PERMIS-
sion, with courtesy and understanding, to publish Daria's
letters. For this I am grateful.

In 1997 I published the book I mentioned about Daria's
father and his three brothers, *The Brothers Hambourg*, without Michal's cooperation. It was published by Robin Brass
in Toronto. Daria and members of her generation were
not mentioned.

Daria never published the novel she was writing in 1947.
The one book that carries her name—"that nobody takes
any notice of"—is the monograph of Richard Doyle, who
had designed the cover of *Punch*.

Her letters are deposited with my papers in the archives
of York University in Toronto.

No names have been changed. Only Lilli Wollstein in
the Ascona chapter is a composite invention.

Some of the material first appeared in *I Remember the Location Exactly* (Mosaic Press, 2006). For this, I have permission from the publisher.

Five weeks after we met, in her fifth letter to me, Daria improvised her own obituary:

September 14, 1938
Obituary on D.H. (Sunday Times)
She rushed through life in great agitation, pursuing her elusive ideals, oblivious to all else, prim in her determination to preserve them intact. On her death bed, the possessive instinct which had been so strongly transmitted to her through her ancestors overwhelmed her at last. In front of astonished spectators assembled to benefit from her will (1 1/2-d stamp, a bunch of feathers and two or three seashells), she staggered to her feet, triumphantly brandished in their faces a cardboard receptacle inscribed "Ideals & Principles," and, with a wild shriek—"They are mine, I will take them with me!"—fell back and expired.